Marco Chiarini
Director of the Pitti Palace

PITTI PALACE
Art and History

Palatine Gallery - Museo degli Argenti - State Apartments - Gallery of Modern Art - Boboli Gardens

Edizioni d'Arte
BECOCCI EDITORE
Via Canto dei Nelli 10/r
Firenze

Index

The Palatine Gallery

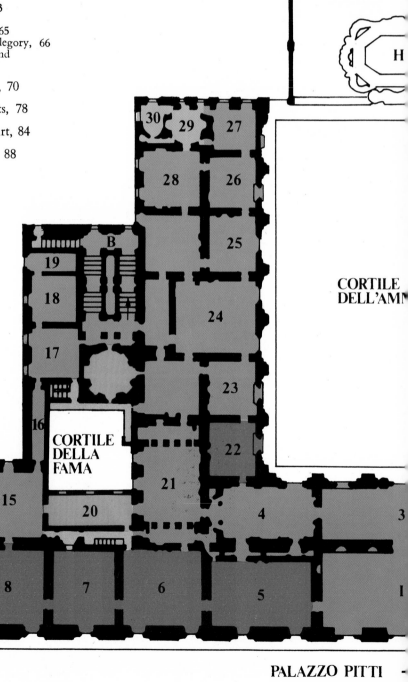

CORTILE DELLA FAMA

CORTILE DELL'AMM

PALAZZO PITTI

Colour Code
Pink - 16th century
Orange - early 17th century
Red - Baroque (full 17th century)
Purple - Rococo (mid-18th century)
Blue - Empire (early 19th century)
Green - late Neoclassicism (1st half 19th century)

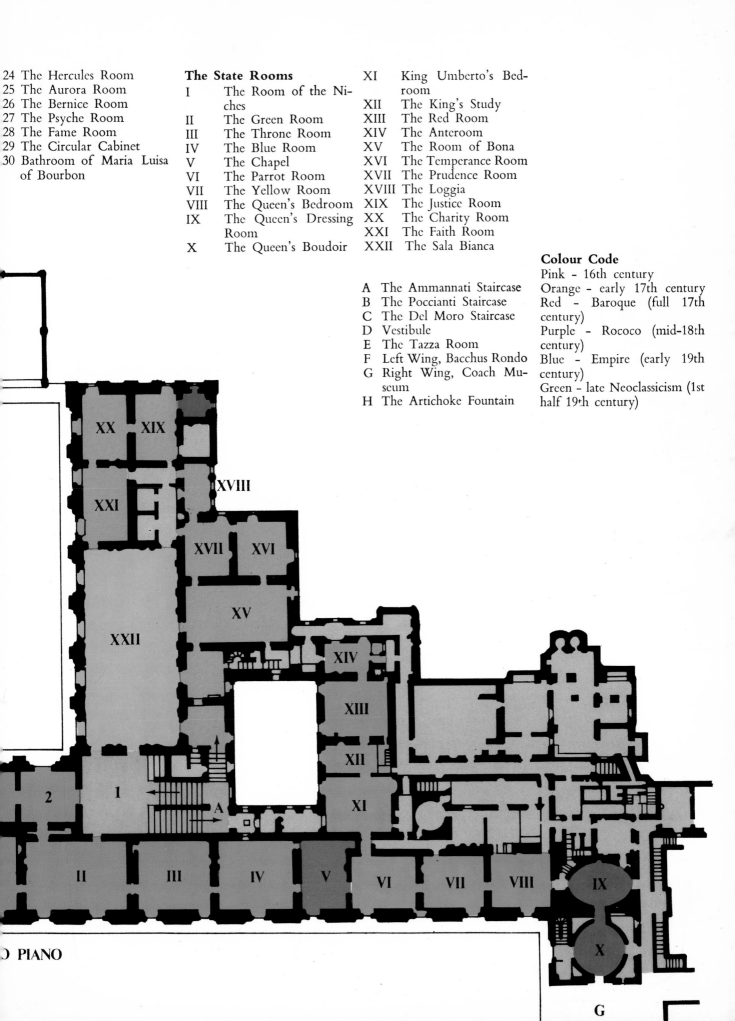

PIANO

G

Introduction

When Luca Pitti died in 1472, the large palace he had built for himself on the slopes of Boboli, south of the Arno, remained unfinished. Unique for its time and « of such size and magnificence that a more exceptional or magnificent Tuscan edifice has yet to be seen » (Vasari), it is not known for certain who was responsible for its design, although Brunelleschi's name is traditionally associated with it and Vasari records that Luca Fancelli supervised the early stages of the building. The palace was acquired in 1550 by Eleonora of Toledo, wife of Cosimo de' Medici, on her husband's advice, and subsequently became the official residence of the Medici rulers. Afterwards, it passed with the Grand Duchy of Tuscany to the House of Lorraine and, finally, on the unification of Italy, to the Royal House of Savoy; consequently, during the course of three centuries, the palace underwent radical changes in size and appearance. The façade of Luca Pitti's palace consisted of two upper floors each with seven windows and three doors on the ground floor (its original appearance is recorded in a few paintings, such as the lunette by Justus Utens, reproduced here), which was later modified when the side doors were replaced by large pedimented windows above lion heads with the Grand-Ducal crown. The garden front was completely altered after 1560 on the construction of the grandiose court with a loggia on three sides and a terrace closing it towards the garden on the fourth. The courtyard, like the fifteenth-century façade of the palace, is built in enormous blocks of roughly hewn stone (the so-called Florentine bugnato) with key-stones of the arches decorated with grotesque masks and rams' heads (one of Cosimo I's emblems). The architect was Bartolomeo Ammannati (1511-1592). Cosimo I's intention of transforming the Pitti Palace into a suburban royal palace is confirmed by the fact that he wished to connect it to the centre of Florentine political life, the Palazzo Vecchio, by means of a corridor built by Giorgio Vasari, which passes over the Ponte Vecchio and through the Uffizi, then also in the course of being built. Plans to enlarge the palace front and arrange the square were finally put into execution under Cosimo II (died 1621) by the architects Giulio and Alfonso Parigi. The façade now assumed its present aspect except for the two wings or rondo, based on a pre-existing plan, which were added by the Lorraine Grand Dukes but only completed in the first half of the nineteenth century (by G. M. Paoletti and P. Poccianti). The same architects also built the Meridiana Palace which forms the continuation of the palace on the south side. Apart from the building of the courtyard by Ammannati, the most important changes which gave the palace its unique character

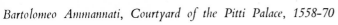

Justus Utens: Lunette in tempera with a view of the Pitti Palace in 1599. Florence, Museo Topografico Fiorentino

Bartolomeo Ammannati, Courtyard of the Pitti Palace, 1558-70

Pietro da Cortona: Sacrifice of Noah, frescoed oval on the mezzanine floor of the Pitti Palace (c. 1644)

Sebastiano Ricci: Venus and Cupid, frescoed ceiling in a ground-floor room of the Pitti Palace

were the interior decorations given to the State Rooms during Medici rule which constitute some of the finest pictorial cycles of seventeenth-century Italian art. Under Ferdinand I and Cosimo II certain rooms were decorated in late-Mannerist style (Poccetti Gallery and Room of Bona, frescoed by Bernardino Poccetti, 1548-1612). However, it was only after Ferdinand's marriage to Vittoria della Rovere (1634), the princess from Urbino whose dowry enriched the Florentine collections with great masterpieces of painting, that the real decorative campaign started, beginning with the ground-floor rooms of the left wing. The frescoes glorifying Lorenzo the Magnificent in the large hall were begun by Giovanni da San Giovanni in 1636 and completed by his followers (Francesco Furini, Cecco Bravo and Ottavio Vannini), and the three following rooms were painted with illusionistic architecture by the Bolognese quadraturisti, Agostino Mitelli and Angelo Michele Colonna (1636-1641).

Salvator Rosa: Finding of Moses, frescoed lunette on the mezzanine floor of the Pitti Palace (c. 1644)

But the most splendid series of decorations were those executed by Pietro Berrettini da Cortona (1596-1669), one of the geniuses of Baroque art, in the former Grand-Ducal State Rooms on the first floor now those of the Palatine Gallery. Pietro da Cortona came to Florence, in 1637 and began painting the Sala della Stufa — the ceiling of which had been completed by the Florentine Matteo Rosselli (1578-1651) in 1622 — and from 1641 to 1647 worked on the most complex cycle of the palace, which comprised the decoration of seven of the front rooms, but which remained unfinished on the artist's final departure from Florence. The Saturn Room was executed entirely by his pupil Ciro Ferri. The art of Pietro da Cortona (who also decorated some mezzanine rooms in collaboration with Salvator Rosa) was to make a profound impression on Florentine painting, evident, for instance, in the ceiling fresco by Volterrano (1611-1689) of the Room of the Allegories in the apartment of Vittoria della Rovere, while the cycles painted by the Florentine Antonio Domenico Gabbiani in other parts of the palace are proof of how this style had become established in the late-seventeenth century. The next decoration of importance was that painted by Sebastiano Ricci (1659-1734), the Venetian artist, in a small room on the ground floor (now the premises of the Soprintendenza ai Monumenti), which formed part of Prince Ferdinand de' Medici's summer apartment: it is one of his most brilliant and attractive creations (1706) and important for the subsequent development of Florentine painting in the eighteenth century. The succession of the House of Hapsburg-Lorraine resulted in radical changes in the decoration of many parts of the palace in keeping with late-eighteenth century Neoclassical taste. On Ferdinand III's return after the Napoleonic interregnum — during which several rooms were decorated in Empire style such as the two bathrooms of Marie Louise, Queen of Etruria — and under his son Leopold II, the interior of the palace, in particular the State Rooms (now the State Apartments) were further transformed so that they lost their seventeenth-century character. Eventually the Grand Duke moved to other wings of the palace, and in 1828 the front rooms painted by Pietro da Cortona became used exclusively for the picture gallery.

Pietro da Cortona: The Continence of Seleucus, frescoed lunette in the Venus Room (c. 1641). This is one of a series of frescoes showing figures from antiquity famous for their continence. Seleucus, the king, renounces his wife to a young man who is dying of love for her.

Palatine Gallery

The picture gallery of the Pitti Palace, known as the Palatine Gallery because it is housed in the royal palace, was opened to the public by Leopold II in 1828. Unlike the Uffizi it always had the character of a private collection and this accounts for the impression of sumptuousness, which is created by the baroque style of some of the decoration and by the very rich frames, many of which date from the time of the first collectors of the paintings, the Medici. While preserving the most important parts of the decoration, Leopold II wished to arrange the collection according to the tastes of his time, and this is also reflected in the choice of works. A number of important paintings were assembled at the Pitti which represented the ideals of classical perfection of the period, among them eleven paintings by Raphael (three were bought during Lorraine reign: the Madonna of the Grand Duke and the Doni portraits), fifteen by Andrea del Sarto and ten by Titian. Other paintings by minor artists were added later. Although the present arrangement corresponds only partially to that given by the Lorraine Grand Dukes, it does, nevertheless, convey the intention of realizing a picture gallery on the lines of the great seventeenth-century princely collections: this explains why the pictures are not arranged according to date or school. These rooms were also provided with a number of sculptures (Canova, Bartolini), and Neoclassical furniture. The access to the Gallery is from the main staircase built by Ammannati in the right-hand corner of the arcade opening onto the courtyard, through the Statue Gallery and the Room of the Niches to the Venus Room, the first of the series of rooms leading to the audience chamber of the Medici Grand Dukes. At the end of the nineteenth century the entrance to the Gallery was moved to the garden side, making use of a wing of the palace which had remained unfinished at the fall of the Lorraine dynasty (1859). The rooms of the so-called Volterrano Apartment, which had formed part of the ruling family's private suite, only came to form part of the picture gallery in 1915. They were hung with paintings mostly from the Uffizi collection, in exchange for which the Palatine Gallery parted with several of its masterpieces (for instance, the Madonna of the Long Neck by Parmigianino, the Rabbi and Self-Portrait as an Old Man by Rembrandt, Leo X and his Nephews by Raphael, etc.).

The Venus Room

RADIX·AMARA VIRTUTIS·FRUCTUS SUAVIS

ADOLESCENTIAM
PALLAS·A·VENERE
AVELLIT

This room originally formed the entrance to the Grand-Ducal apartment in the time of Ferdinand II.
It was here that Pietro da Cortona began the series of allegorical frescoes alluding to the
life of an idealized Prince, who is here represented torn away from the arms of Venus by Pallas Athena in
order to be received by Hercules and prepared for his mission. The stucco decoration of the ceiling,
also by Pietro da Cortona, is exceptionally elaborate: besides the gilded telamons which appear to
support part of the decoration there are four large medallions containing portraits of the most outstanding figures of the
Medici family from the sixteenth century onwards: Cosimo I and Francesco I, Popes Leo X and Clement VII,
Ferdinand I and Cosimo II, Ferdinand II and his small son, Cosimo III.

Titian

Titian, The Concert, detail (oil on canvas, 109 × 123 cm.). This painting was acquired by Cardinal Leopold de' Medici as a work by Giorgione. Although this attribution has never been abandoned, the name of Titian is now more usually accepted. Whether by Giorgione or by Titian in his Giorgionesque phase, this

Titian

Tiziano Vecellio, called Titian (Pieve di Cadore, c. 1490-Venice, 1576). Portrait of a Woman, known as La Bella (oil on canvas, 69 x 75 cm.). This is one of the Venetian artist's most famous female portraits; but the subject's identity remains a mystery. It is known that the portrait was painted by Titian for the Duke of Urbino in 1536. The whole painting is dominated by the woman's beauty, her magnificent dark eyes and perfectly shaped mouth: she may be the woman who posed for the Venus of Urbino at the Uffizi, whose beauty represents an ideal of perfection.

painting is a masterpiece of the fundamental moment in the development of Venetian, and consequently European painting which began with Giorgione in the first years of the sixteenth century in Venice. Typically Giorgionesque is the intense psychological vitality of these three figures, who have just ended their concert; also the theme inherent in the vibrating figure of the harpsichord player in the centre, whose inspired expression and sensitive hands, restlessly fingering the keyboard, hold the spectator's attention; and the tonality of the colours, in their blended browns, blacks, greys and whites.

Titian

Titian, Portrait of Pietro Aretino, detail (oil on canvas, 108 × 76 cm.). Of the many portraits by Titian in the Pitti Gallery this is one of the most striking and most powerful. It was painted in 1545, as we know from a letter sent by Aretino, the famous Venetian scholar and friend of rulers and artists, to Cosimo I de' Medici in which he offered him the painting, justly accepted by Cosimo. It is a superb example of how Titian's style becomes progressively more painterly and free. Even though, from a distance, the figure appears compact and three-dimensionally « drawn », from close to one finds that the painted surface is broken up into innumerable touches of colour, and strokes of paint applied directly onto the canvas with a pre-Impressionistic feeling for the medium.

Titian

Titian, Portrait of Pope Julius II (oil on panel, 99 × 82 cm.). Julius II della Rovere commissioned Raphael to paint his portrait shortly before his death in a famous work which remained for a long time in S. Maria del Popolo in Rome and now hangs in the National Gallery in London (numerous replicas and copies are known, one of which is in the Uffizi). Titian saw Raphael's painting in Rome and made this copy of it for the Duke of Urbino. Although it does not achieve the force of the original it is, nevertheless, an intelligent and personal translation, which does not betray the spirit of the original. Particularly fine is Titian's free brushwork, which gives the colour delicacy and brilliance.

Salvator Rosa

Salvator Rosa (Naples, 1615 - Rome, 1673). Seascape at Sunset (oil on canvas, 233 × 399 cm.). Rosa was active at the court of the Medici for almost ten years (1640-49) where he painted works congenial to the tastes of his patrons: battle scenes, landscapes, seascapes, allegorical scenes (now mostly in the Psyche Room). This large seascape, which forms a pendant to the painting on the opposite wall (both painted for Cardinal Carlo de' Medici) shows Rosa under the influence of the great French landscapist, Claude Lorrain (see Harbour at Sunset in the Uffizi) in the effect of light falling on the sea and in the hazy atmosphere of a golden sunset; but his own very marked personality comes out in the figure groups animating the scene which are observed with a sharp realism typical of the Neapolitan artist.

Rubens

Peter Paul Rubens (Siegen, 1577-Antwerp, 1640), Peasants Returning from the Fields (oil on panel, 121.5 × 194 cm.). Rubens was also a great landscape painter: the Pitti has two important examples of this genre, the second being Ulysses on the Island of Phaeacia, of which this painting forms the pendant. The artist succeeds in evoking the life of peasants in his country with a wealth of detail and feeling of spaciousness inspired by the natural scenery of the Netherlands. The golden light of a summer sunset bathes the vast plain bringing out the details of the plants, the reflections in the stream and the play of light on the bundles of hay and grass carried by the figures, thereby revealing an attention to detail and a sense of intimate familiarity with nature typical of Dutch painters.

Rubens' observation of nature is documented by his numerous drawings from life in black chalk, in which he recorded details for inclusion in his paintings: trees, animals, studies of plants, etc., which enable us to follow his creative process. Another painting, similar to this work in its composition and sunset atmosphere, is the famous Landscape with a Rainbow in the Pinakothek in Munich.

LIST OF PAINTINGS NOT REPRODUCED

Bassano, F. the younger, *Martyrdom of St. Catherine*. Bilivert, G., *Apollo and Marsyas*. Bonifacio Veronese, *Madonna and Child with Saints*. Cantarini, S., *St. Isidor*. Cigoli, *Christ's third apparition to St. Peter*. Emilian School, 16th century, *Portrait said to be of Torquato Tasso*. Gambara, L., *Deposition*. Guercino, *Apollo and Marsyas; St. Joseph*. Manetti, R., *Ruggero and Alcina*. Passarotti, B., *Portrait of Guidobaldo della Rovere*. Pietro da Cortona, *St. Martina*. Piombo, S. del, *Portrait of Baccio Valori*. Reni, G., *Portrait of an old Man*. Rosa, S., *Falsehood; Seascape with Boats and Galley*. Rosselli, M., *Triumph of David*. Rubens, P. P., *Ulysses on the Island of Phaeacia*. Sustermans, J., *Huntsmen Feasting*. Tintoretto, J., *Venus, Vulcan and Cupid*. Vanni, R., *Mystic Marriage of St. Catherine*. Venetian School, 16th century, *Madonna and Child with two Angels*.

The Apollo Room

The fresco dominating the ceiling by Pietro da Cortona (1647) represents the young Prince conversing with Apollo, protector of the Arts and Sciences (symbolized by the surrounding figures, shown in bold foreshortening). This fresco, like those in the spandrels and cartouches, was completed by Pietro's pupil, Ciro Ferri. The elaborate stucco framework of this room is particularly fine and has oval medallions containing white figures against a gold ground representing episodes from the story of Apollo.

Rosso Fiorentino

Giovanni Battista di Jacopo, called Rosso Fiorentino (Florence, 1494-1540), Madonna Enthroned with Saints (oil on panel, 350 × 259 cm.). Signed and dated 1522, this painting was acquired in the seventeenth century from the Florentine church of S. Spirito. It was then that the painting was enlarged to its present size (the additions are clearly visible at the joins in the wood). This is a typical work of Florentine Mannerism of which Rosso was one of the most original exponents. Compared with Cinquecento classicism the composition is crowded and contracted towards the background, while the unnaturally fragmented forms are underlined by transparent, changing colours that become unreal and stress the strange atmosphere of this « Sacra Conversazione ».

Titian

Titian, Portrait of a Man in Black, detail (oil on canvas, 113 × 96 cm.). The identity of the sitter still remains a mystery: he has been variously called the Duke of Norfolk (hence the title, The Englishman), the Ferrarese jurist Ippolito Riminaldi and other equally unsubstantiated names. The most striking feature of his beautiful and noble countenance is his grey-blue eyes (the portrait is also known as the Man with the Grey Eyes); his face is the focal point of the composition and all the other details are merely complementary. Even the beautiful hands, like the collar and cuffs of his shirt, accentuate the subtle harmony of greys and blacks which provide a foil to the golden tonality of his face; and it is this quality that makes this portrait one of the masterpieces of sixteenth-century Venetian painting.

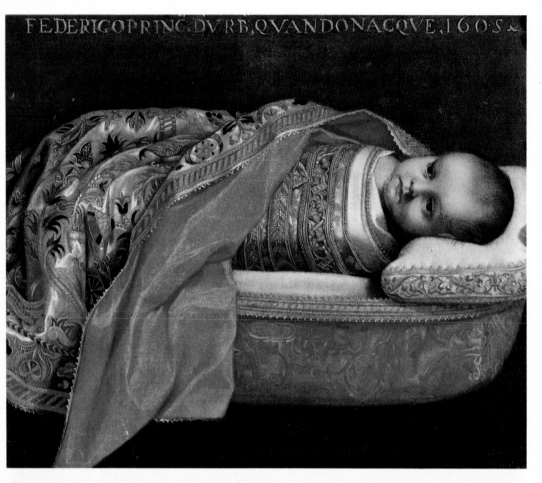

Baroccio

Federico Baroccio (Urbino, 1535-1612), Portrait of Federico of Urbino in his Cradle (oil on canvas, 60 × 73 cm.). This painting with its beautifully rendered details (the cover, the cradle, trimmings and the embroidery of the cushion) shows with what immediacy the artist was capable of evoking the impression of a child and with a feeling for colour that is a constant factor in Barocci's work.

Cigoli

Ludovico Cardi, called Cigoli (S. Miniato, 1559 - Rome, 1613), Portrait of a Man, detail (oil on canvas, 55 × 42 cm.). Cigoli's art concludes the great Florentine tradition of religious and monumental painting. He is represented in the Gallery by several important works (Deposition, Stoning of St. Stephen, St. Francis receiving the Stigmata in the Fine Arts Room; Christ appearing to St. Peter in the Venus Room). However we have preferred to represent him by one of his finest portraits, this Man in Black, which conveys particularly well the analytical and introspective character of his art and his extremely refined use of colour in the simple blending of blacks, whites and browns.

Titian

Titian, The Magdalen (oil on panel, 84 × 69 cm.). The painting is signed on the ointment jar on the left. It was painted for the Duke of Urbino around 1531, and is recorded by Vasari as « a rare work ». The execution is remarkable, both in the rendering of the blue sky and of the silken hair and glowing flesh tones. This image of the Saint was to become a favorite interpretation in sixteenth century painting and the prototype of numerous workshop copies.

Anthony van Dyck

Anthony van Dyck (Antwerp, 1599-London, 1641), Portrait of Charles I of England and his Wife, Henrietta Maria of France (oil on canvas, 66 × 82 cm.). This painting is a double portrait of Charles I, beheaded in London in 1649, and of his wife Henrietta Maria, daughter of Henry IV and Maria de' Medici. The artist has concentrated especially on the psychological characterization of the sitters: the king melancholy and almost romantic; the queen more self-conscious and ironical. The rendering of the lace and jewels decorating the dress and armour is particularly fine.

LIST OF PAINTINGS NOT REPRODUCED
Allori, C., *Hospitality of St. Julian.* Barocci, F., *Portrait of Federigo, Prince of Urbino as a Child.* Cantarini, S., *St. Andrew.* Cassana, N., *Portrait of a Warrior.* Cigoli, *Portrait of a Man.* Crayer, C. de, *Holy Family.* Dolci, C., *Diogenes; St. Casimir; St. John the Evangelist.* Dossi, D., *Nymph and Satyr; St. John the Baptist.* Emilian School, 17th century, *Portrait of a Man.* Empoli, *Madonna of Mercy.* Flemish School, 17th century, *Portait of a Man.* Garofalo, *Sibyl revealing the Mystery of the Incarnation.* Guercino, *Raising of Tabitha.* Ligozzi, J., *Judith.* Mazzolino, L., *The Adultress.* Morales, L. de (School of), *Ecce Homo.* Palma il Vecchio, (school of), *Supper at Emmaus.* Roman School, 17th century, *Portrait of Donna Olimpia Aldobrandini.* Rosa, S., *Portrait of an old Man.* Rubens, P. P., *Portrait of Isabella Clara Eugenia, Governess of the Netherlands.* Sarto, A. del, *Holy Family with St. Elizabeth; Holy Family; Deposition; Portrait of a young Man.* Sustermans, J., *Portrait of Cosimo III as a Child; Portrait of Vittoria della Rovere as the Vestal Virigin Tutia.* Tintoretto, J., *Portrait of Vincenzo Zeno.* Titi, T., *Portrait of Leopold de' Medici as a Baby.* Titian (school of), *Madonna and Child with Saints; Madonna of Mercy.* Vos, C. de, *Portrait of Woman with a Fan.*

The Mars Room

This is the only room frescoed by Pietro da Cortona in which there is a clear allusion to the ruling family: the Medici arms dominate the centre of the ceiling, surmounted by the Grand Ducal crown engraved with the name of Ferdinand II who commissioned the frescoes. Unlike the other rooms, only the actual ceiling is decorated with frescoes without other paintings beneath the frame. The theme is the glorification of the prince's warrior virtues: Mars flies down to set fire to a naval combat while Victories carry arms to Hercules; beyond, prisoners pay homage to Victory crowned with laurel.

Titian

Titian, Portrait of Ippolito de' Medici, detail (oil on canvas, 138 × 106 cm.). The natural son of Giuliano, Duke of Nemours (whose tomb was carved by Michelangelo for the New Sacristy of S. Lorenzo) Ippolito was made a cardinal by Clement VII (also a Medici) in 1529. However, he never took orders and in 1533 he defended Vienna with four thousand harquebusiers against the Turks. On his return to Italy he wished to have his portrait painted by Titian « in Hungarian dress » (Vasari). It is an unusually large-scale portrait for Titian but, at the same time, extremely subtle in the tonal range of greys and purples which set off the pale face of the young prince whose noble bearing is well suited to his Hungarian Magnate dress.

Veronese

Paolo Caliari, called Veronese (Verona, 1528 - Venice, 1588), Portrait of a Man (oil on canvas, 140 × 107 cm.). The unknown subject of this picture has sometimes been erroneously identified as Daniele Barbaro, the Venetian patrician and humanist. It is one of Veronese's most impressive portraits. The sober blend of greys and blacks act as a foil to the fur and the ruddy features with their proud and vivid expression.

Rubens ▶

Peter Paul Rubens, The Four Philosophers (oil on panel, 164 × 139 cm.). In this famous painting Rubens portrayed himself (left, standing), his brother Philip (wearing a ruff), the philosopher Justus Lipsius (Philip's teacher) and, in the right foreground, Jan van der Wouwère, another of Lipsius' pupils. The red velvet curtain behind them opens onto a landscape; to the right in a niche is a marble bust of Seneca with a vase of tulips. This painting, which was certainly meant to commemorate Lipsius' teaching, is unusually large and important for a group portrait dating from the first years of the seventeenth century. Besides its rich colouring, this work is characterized by exquisitely painted details such as the still life of books and quill pens on the table or the vase of tulips above.

Rubens

Peter Paul Rubens, The Consequences of War (oil on canvas, 206 × 345 cm.). This masterpiece, dating from the Flemish painter's last years (1638), was sent by him as a gift to his close friend Justus Sustermans, portrait painter to the Medici. On Susterman's death it passed into the Medici collection. This work illustrates the two principal stylistic trends of the artist: love of vibrant, sensual and rich colours and of forms in constant movement. Venus is shown trying to hold back Mars as he sets off to war, the catastrophical consequences of which are visible both in the trampled pages of a book, an illusion to the ruin war causes culture and the arts, and in the despairing figures on the right. The inspiration of Venetian painting, and of Titian and Paolo Veronese in particular, is evident, especially in the rendering of the female nudes and children with their pearly flesh tones and shining golden hair.

Murillo ◄

Bartolomé Esteban Murillo (Seville, 1618-1682), Madonna and Child, detail (oil on canvas, 157 × 107 cm.). Together with the other painting of the same subject hanging nearby, this is a typical work by the Sevillian artist who was famous for his pious images of great devotion and sweetness. Especially notable are the soft, blended colours and the life-like expressions of Mother and Child, which are rendered with an inner humanity peculiar to this type of Spanish religious painting.

Anthony van Dyck

Anthony van Dyck, Portrait of Cardinal Guido Bentivoglio, detail (oil on canvas, 195 × 147 cm.). This painting reveals Van Dyck's cultural formation: he combines the basic inspiration of Venetian art, and of Titian in particular, with the richness and brilliance of colour typical of his master, Rubens. Van Dyck became one of the most famous portrait painters in Europe, acclaimed and sought after by the aristocracy. Charles I of England invited him to court and made him his official painter. Compared with Rubens' portraits, those of van Dyck lay less emphasis on the character of the sitter than on his social status and official aspect. This superb portrait, done when the artist was still strongly under the influence of Italian art, was probably painted in 1623 (Cardinal Bentivoglio came from an important Bolognese family and was papal ambassador in Flanders and France). The various nuances of red enhance the sitter's luminous and aristocratic features and his sensitive hands; while the white lace of his cardinal's robes animates the figure at the centre of the painting. Also extremely beautiful is the still-life of papers and the vase of flowers on the table.

The Jupiter Room

The Grand Ducal throne originally stood in this room and it
is here that visitors were given
audience. The ceiling is superbly
decorated with frescoes and stucco
work by Pietro da Cortona (1643-
1646). The Baroque ideal of
spatial illusionism is achieved
here in the garlandlike arrangement of the figures adapted to
the circular frame which creates
the impression of a stage for the
scene: some of the figures lean
forward looking down at the
spectator. The allegorical intention is clear: Jupiter welcomes to
Olympus the young prince presented to him by Hercules and
Victory, symbols of the moral
virtues of the heir to the throne.
The decoration of this room forms
the culminating point in the
sequence of the seven front rooms,
corresponding to seven planets,
planned by Pietro da Cortona,
but left unfinished. The grandiose fresco is remarkable for
the atmospheric quality and tran-
sparency of its colouring and for
the diffused light which really
succeeds in evoking the optical
effect of an opening towards the
sky. Beside this room is a small
frescoed chapel, separated by an
opening in the wall with gold
bars for the Grand Duke's private
devotions, which is now hidden
by the material lining the walls
and the large painting of St Mark
by Fra Bartolomeo.

Bronzino

Agnolo di Cosimo, called Bronzino (Florence, 1503-1572), Portrait of Guidobaldo della Rovere (oil on panel, 114 × 86 cm.). Bronzino was the official portrait painter of Cosimo I de' Medici and his family; his portraits of Eleonora of Toledo and their children, now in the Uffizi, are among his finest works. Bronzino was a pupil of Pontormo whose stylized elegance he interpreted particularly in terms of brilliant enamelled colours. In this portrait, however, the range of colours is rather subdued and attention is concentrated on the rendering of the extremely rich damascened armour, set against the dark green ground which acts as a foil to the pale, aristocratic face of this eighteen-year-old prince of Urbino.

Piero del Pollaiolo

Piero del Pollaiolo (Florence, 1443-1496), St. Jerome (oil on panel, 40 × 26 cm.). The attribution to Piero del Pollaiolo of this powerfully characterized head of a saint goes back to the seventeenth-century inventory of the Medici collection. Nevertheless, it differs to some extent from the artist's authenticated works, and the name of Piero's more gifted brother, Antonio, has been suggested. Although the attribution remains uncertain, this work is a typical example of Florentine painting between 1450 and 1470 when anatomical studies, especially those of Antonio, were progressing towards a boldness present in the synthetic foreshortening of this head.

Raphael

Raffaello Sanzio, called Raphael (Urbino, 1483-Rome, 1520), Portrait of a Woman, known as La Velata (oil on canvas, 85 × 64 cm.). This famous portrait was regarded as by an anonymous artist until the last century: today it is universally accepted as one of the masterpieces of Raphael's Roman period (c. 1516). The beautiful young woman, sometimes identified as the fictitious Fornarina, who is supposed to have been his mistress, is richly dressed and adorned with jewels which point to her belonging to an aristocratic family. Her veil envelops her creating the effect of a half-opened shell. The sober range of colours underlines the warmth of her expression and the palpitating quality of her complexion. The puffed sleeve is a magnificent piece of painting which only Titian could equal. The purity of line of this classical figure was to remain an unforgettable example at least until the nineteenth century, when the French painter Ingres seems to have found in her the inspiration for his ideal in painting.

Fra' Bartolomeo

Bartolomeo della Porta, called Fra Bartolomeo (Florence, 1472-1517), The Lamentation over the Dead Christ
(oil on panel, 158 × 199 cm.). Fra Bartolomeo's strong personality is fully conveyed in this
Lamentation, his last work, left partly unfinished in the background (it has been heavily repainted in the past).
The composition stretches from the compact group of the Madonna and St. John
supporting Christ's body to the kneeling figure of the Magdalen at his feet: a simple geometric
rhythm, emphasized by the deep tones of red, blue and orange. The perfect drawing, warm tonality and certain bold
foreshortenings must have been admired by Raphael, whose art owed so much
to that of Fra Bartolomeo.
In its accomplished drawing — note especially the anatomy of Christ's body and the foreshortening of the Magdalen —
and balance of volumes this work achieves a formal perfection that is combined with an intense spiritual impact.

Anonymous Giorgionesque

Anonymous Giorgionesque artist, early sixteenth century, The Three Ages of Man (oil on panel, 62 × 77 cm.). The extremely high quality of this painting, despite its poor condition, has always accounted for its attribution to great Venetian artists such as Giovanni Bellini and Giorgione. Whereas the name of the former is less likely by virtue of the marked sixteenth-century character of the painting, that of Giorgione (d. 1510) is acceptable. The fusion of colours in this painting is unparalleled in Bellini's works of that date, and the psychological penetration, the expressive force of the faces and certain physiological types are those that recur in the works of Giorgione, to whose circle this masterpiece of the first years of the sixteenth century belongs.

Andrea del Sarto

Andrea d'Agnolo, called Andrea del Sarto (Florence, 1486-1530), St. John the Baptist as a Boy (oil on panel, 94 × 68 cm.). This painting belonged to Cosimo I de' Medici and hung in the Tribuna of the Uffizi. It is one of the most celebrated images of this saint, famous for the idealized beauty of the figure, the powerful draughtsmanship and the originality of the composition. The drawing of the nude is entirely unselfconscious; it is observed realistically but becomes abstract through the artist's typical stylization of form. The background of the painting has suffered as a result of previous cleanings.

Perugino

Pietro Vannucci, called Perugino (Città della Pieve, c. 1450-1523), Madonna Adoring the Christ Child, called Madonna of the Sack (oil on panel, 88 × 86 cm.). This picture derives its name from the sack on which the infant Jesus is seated held up by an angel. The devotional image here blends harmoniously with the landscape which opens out to either side in converging lines which accentuate the Madonna's primary role in the composition. The predominant light blue tints and the beauty of the drawing contrast with the flesh tones and certain less delicate passages which may well be the work of assistants.

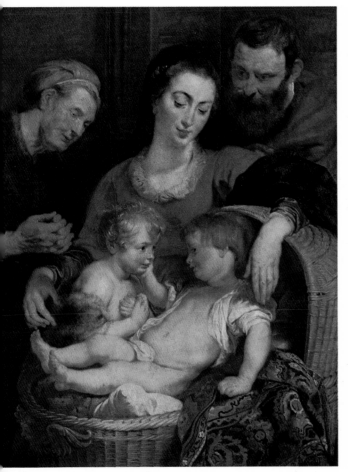

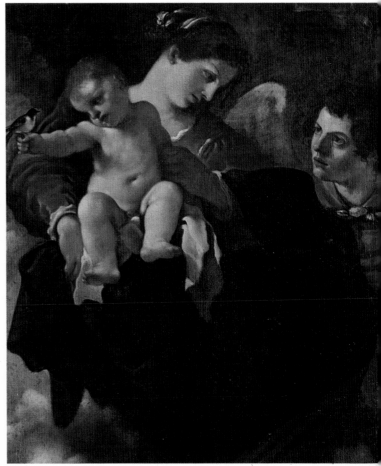

Rubens

Peter Paul Rubens, The Holy Family of the Basket (oil on panel, 114 × 88 cm.). Rubens is represented by several of his masterpieces, which give an idea of the rich and exuberant personality of this supreme northern interpreter of Baroque taste. In this painting, the impetus which characterizes the works of the painter from Antwerp becomes subdued in a serene and intimate scene of a family around the cradle of a small child. Among Rubens' many accomplishments is his capacity to render the mother's gentle expression, the fresh flesh tones and golden hair and such details as the vividly coloured blanket on the right.

Guercino

Giovan Francesco Barbieri, called Guercino (Cento, 1591 - Bologna, 1666), Madonna of the Swallow (oil on canvas, 120 × 88 cm.). The Palatine Gallery has several fine early works by Guercino including the other Holy Family in the same room, the Raising of Tabitha in the Apollo Room and Apollo flaying Marsyas in the Venus Room. In this simple composition, Guercino reveals the qualities typical of his early style: thick brushwork and warm juicy colours blending with an intense use of chiaroscuro derived from Caravaggio.

LIST OF PAINTINGS NOT REPRODUCED
Albani, F., *Holy Family with two Angels; Christ appearing to the Virgin*. Baroccio, F., *The Redeemer*. Bartolomeo, Fra, *St. Mark the Evangelist*. Bassano, J., *Christ before Pilate*. Bordone, P., *Portrait of a Woman*. Borgognone, *Battle Scene*. Caroselli, A. (attributed), *St. Agnes*. Cassana, N., *Conspiracy of Catiline*. Cigoli, *Holy Family*. Dolci, C., *Portrait of young Man of the Bardi Family*. Gennari, C., *Madonna and Child*. Guercino, *Holy Family; Moses*. Lanfranco, G., *Ecstasy of St. Margaret of Cortona*. Perugino, *Madonna and Child with St. John and Angel*. Pourbus the Younger, *Portrait of a young Man*. Reni, G., *St. Elizabeth*. Rubens, P. P., *Nymphs and Satyrs*. Salviati, *The Three Fates*. Sarto, A. del, *Annunciation; Deposition; Madonna in Glory with four Saints*. Schedoni, B., *Holy Family*. Sustermans, J., *Portrait of Elia, Captain of the Tuscan Galleys; Portrait of Simone Pacanucci*. Sustermans, J. (School of), *Portrait of Galileo Galilei*. Venetian School, 16th century, *Portrait of a Man*. Vignali, J., *Ecstasy of St. Francis*.

31

The Saturn Room

This is the last in the original sequence of rooms decorated by Pietro da Cortona (Cortona, 1596 - Rome, 1669). The spatial and decorative conception and the stucco framework reflect this artist's design but the frescoes were executed by his pupil Ciro Ferri (1662-1665). Like the other ceilings of these rooms frescoed with mythological scenes by Pietro da Cortona, this one dedicated to Saturn is an allegorical glorification of the Medici family.

Raphael

Raphael, Portrait of Maddalena Doni (oil on panel, 63 × 45 cm.). This splendid portrait of Maddalena Strozzi forms a pair with that of her husband Agnolo Doni. They were painted a few years after their marriage (1503) possibly in 1505-06. Both portraits, thanks to their excellent state of preservation, give us an idea of the mastery achieved by Raphael in the field of portraiture while still in his early period. The figure of Maddalena is evidently inspired by Leonardo's Mona Lisa, both in her pose and in the way the hands are placed. The teaching of Raphael's first master, Perugino, is visible in the relationship between figure and landscape, in the delicate tones of light blue, and in the masterly balance of volumes. Typical of Raphael is the treatment of the amber-coloured flesh tones, the drawing of the beautiful, sensitive hands, the pictorial rendering of silks and damasks instilled with light and the geometrical treatment of forms, such as the rounded outline of the shoulders and the oval face. Both portraits were acquired for the Pitti Gallery by Leopold II in 1826.

Raphael

Raphael, Madonna and Child known as Madonna of the Grand Duke (oil on panel, 85 × 56 cm.). This painting was acquired by Ferdinand II of Lorraine at the end of the eighteenth century. The Grand Duke was very attached to it — hence the title — so much so that it always hung over his bed and went with him when he travelled. It is not known when Raphael painted this work but it must date from his Florentine period around 1505-6; it is supposed to have belonged to the painter Carlo Dolci. In a series of paintings of the same subject — Washington, London, Munich, Chantilly, etc. — Raphael varied the theme according to a new iconography, inspired primarily by Leonardo da Vinci. Later (Madonna of the Chair) he developed a more complex grouping of the figures articulated in a circular movement.

Perugino

Pietro Vannucci, called Perugino, The Magdalen (oil on panel, 47 × 34 cm.). The Umbrian artist who, as Raphael's master, contributed so much to the formation of the latter's style, is famous for the grace and delicacy of his figures. At the Pitti he is represented by three significant works: this Magdalen, the signed and dated Deposition of 1495, and the Madonna of the Sack. The Magdalen, attributed in the past to Leonardo da Vinci, is an image of particular beauty in its sobriety of conception and deep colours (unusual for Perugino who was fond of light tones) and in the melancholy which haunts the saint's youthful features.

Raphael

Raphael, Madonna and Child with Infant St. John, known as Madonna of the Chair (oil on circular panel, diam. 71 cm.). This is perhaps Raphael's most famous Madonna, and almost the symbol of the Palatine Gallery to which it was transferred from the Tribuna of the Uffizi at the beginning of the eighteenth century. It was already in the Medici collection a few years after Raphael's death. This compact group develops a compositional motif which Raphael had already adopted in a painting now in the Pinakothek in Munich. The Pitti painting dates from the artist's last years, the mid-1510's, when his style reached its utmost maturity and complexity. Here the unusual use of a circular panel, derived from the Florentine tradition (see that of Filippo Lippi in the Prometheus Room), harmonizes perfectly with the circular concept underlying the group which produces a rotatory feeling accentuated by the placing of the figures in depth. The warm colour tones, forming a range of reds, yellows, greens and blues, are also

RAFFAELLO SANZIO

N. AD URBINO 6 APRILE 1183

M. A ROMA 6 APRILE 1520

characteristic of Raphael's later style in which he developed a richer chromatic sense, possibly under the influence of Venetian art.

Jacopo Bassano

Jacopo da Ponte, called Bassano (Bassano, c. 1510-1592), Adam and Eve in the Garden of Eden (oil on panel, 76 × 53.5 cm.). Of the numerous Bassanesque paintings in the Gallery, this is the only one that can be attributed to the major painter of the da Ponte family, Jacopo, one of the greatest Venetian artists of the sixteenth century. Known primarily for his biblical subjects, Jacopo introduced into his religious composition details derived from his study of life, nature and animals. This painting also illustrates his taste for rich colours and his realistic rendering of the nude. Another painting of the same subject is in the Doria Gallery in Rome.

Carlo Dolci

Carlo Dolci (Florence, 1616-1686), Infant St. John asleep (oil on canvas, oval, 45 × 58 cm.). Famous for his religious images, of which there are a number at the Pitti, Dolci painted devotional works for Vittoria della Rovere, wife of Ferdinand II de' Medici, of which this is one. A brilliant colourist (see St. John on Patmos in the Ulysses Room and the fine Martyrdom of St. Andrew in the Education of Jupiter Room), the artist here makes use of the dominant blacks and greys to accentuate the austere and pious character of this work.

Ridolfo del Ghirlandaio

Ridolfo Bigordi, called Ridolfo del Ghirlandaio (Florence, 1483-1561). Portrait of a Man, known as the Goldsmith (oil on panel, 43.5 × 31.5 cm.). Son of the more famous Domenico Ghirlandaio, Ridolfo was a fine portraitist; in fact, the Goldsmith (so-called because the sitter is portrayed examining a jewel) was at one time attributed to Leonardo da Vinci. The artist's accomplishment in this genre is also illustrated by the fine Portrait of a Woman (1509) hanging in the Iliad Room. Ridolfo was influenced by various artists including Leonardo and Raphael without, however, equalling them in the rendering of form or psychological subtlety.

Raphael

Raphael, Portrait of Cardinal Inghirami (oil on panel, 90 × 62 cm.). Cardinal Inghirami, known as Fedra, was born at Volterra: he held important posts at the papal court of Leo X de' Medici. This portrait dates from shortly before 1516, the year of the cardinal's death. It is a powerful work in which the artist achieves a symphony of reds prompted by the prelate's robes and a compactness of form underlined by the purity of the drawing. Raphael also attains an extraordinary subtlety of execution in the plump hands, the book and inkwell which, together with the acute analysis of the cardinal's features, support the authenticity of this version as opposed to that in the Gardner Museum in Boston.

LIST OF PAINTINGS NOT REPRODUCED
Bartolomeo, Fra, *The Risen Christ with the Evangelists*. Bassano, J., *Adam and Eve*. Bassano, L., *Pastoral Scene*. Caracci, A., *Head of a Man*. Dolci, C., *Moses; Portrait of Vittoria della Rovere; St. Margaret; St. Rose of Lima*. Empoli, *Portrait of G. B. Gambetti*. Florentine School, 16th century, *Portrait of a Woman*. Giovanni di San Giovanni, *Madonna and Child*. Guercino, *St. Peter; St. Sebastian*. Mola, P. F., *A Poet*. Perugino, *Deposition*. Puligo, D., *Holy Family*. Raphael, *Madonna of the Baldachin; Portrait of Agnolo Doni; Portrait of Cardinal Bernardo Dovizi; Vision of Ezechiel*. Sarto, A. del, *Discussion of the Trinity*. Schiavone, *Samson slaying a Philistine*. Sodoma, *Ecce Homo*. Spagna, *Mystic Marriage of St. Catherine*. Sustermans, J., *Portrait of a Woman; Portrait of Canon Pandolfo Ricasoli*. Tiarini, A., *Adam and Eve mourning the dead Abel*. Titan (School of), *Mystic Marriage of St. Catherine*. Venetian School, 16th century, *Portrait of a Woman with a Book; Portrait of a Woman in Black*.

The Iliad Room

This room, originally called 'dei Novissimi' on account of its having been decorated towards the end of the seventeenth century with biblical stories by Giuseppe Nasini, after Pietro da Cortona had failed to carry out the decoration, was the last of the Grand Ducal rooms at the time of the Medici and gave 'onto a chapel, that has since been destroyed. It was completely altered in the Neoclassical period, beginning in in 1815. The frescoes were painted by Luigi Sabatelli (1772-1850) between 1819 and 1825 with scenes from the Iliad in the lunettes, and Olympus in the central tondo of the ceiling.

Raphael

Raphael, Portrait of a Woman, known as La Gravida (oil on panel, 66 × 52 cm.). This austere portrait represents a pregnant woman (hence the name La Gravida) who, to judge from her hairstyle, dress and jewels, belonged to a wealthy family. It is a work of Raphael's Florentine period (1504-1508) when, after his apprenticeship with Perugino, he transformed his first experience as an artist into a more ample idiom as a result of his study of contemporary Florentine painting, especially that of Leonardo da Vinci and Fra Bartolomeo. Here the light blue tones and open backgrounds of Perugino give way to a simplicity of conception in which all the attention is concentrated on the figure outlined against a dark compact ground. Raphael uses line to emphasize the volumes of the forms which are further enhanced by the colours and their tonal nuances. The extremely high quality of the painting is epitomized in certain details such as the ruby red brocade of the sleeve, the plump hands, the one resting in her lap seen in a synthetic foreshortening which Raphael alone could achieve.

Andrea del Sarto

Andrea del Sarto, The Assumption of the Virgin (oil on panel, 379 × 222 cm.). This is one of the masterpieces of the artist who is represented at the Pitti by a conspicuous group of works. This Assumption, painted around 1527, is based on the composition dating from a few years earlier on the opposite wall. The principal novelty is the monumental rendering of a religious theme which the artist developed under the influence of Fra Bartolomeo. Andrea breaks away from the traditional iconography and succeeds in isolating the heavenly sphere (the Virgin seated on the clouds) from the earthly sphere (the Apostles around the tomb). At the same time, the atmospheric fusion created by the softly blended colours, influenced by Leonardo, which range from subtle variations of tone to shot tints, and the grandiose design in depth and upwards, seem to foreshadow Baroque taste.

Frans Pourbus the Younger

Frans Pourbus the Younger (Antwerp, 1569 - Paris, 1622), Portrait of Eleonora of Mantua as a Girl (oil on canvas, 64 × 49 cm.). Eleonora Gonzaga married the Hapsburg Emperor Ferdinand II in 1622; five years later she was crowned Queen of Bohemia. This portrait of her as a young girl dates from her residence at her father's court, where Pourbus stayed between 1600 and 1609. The artist, famous for his portraits, knew how to render the freshness of the girl's features and gave particular importance to the details of her rich costume, achieving brilliant effects of colour and drawing. In the Iliad Room there is another portrait by Pourbus of this sitter's mother, Eleonora de' Medici.

Artemisia Gentileschi

Artemisia Gentileschi (Rome, 1593 - Naples, 1652), Judith (oil on canvas, 117 × 93 cm.). In this painting, which probably dates from the artist's stay in Florence, Artemisia Gentileschi reveals a thorough understanding of the style of Caravaggio, the great Lombard painter whose use of contrasts of light and shade became a fundamental and characteristic element of his mature works (see the Sleeping Cupid in the Education of Jupiter Room). At the same time, however, Artemisia did not forget the influence of her father, Orazio Gentileschi, a faithful follower of Caravaggesque realism, and, particularly in her use of brilliant whites and yellows, shows a tendency towards delicate optical effects typical of Florentine painting of the seventeenth century. Such a tendency is even more pronounced in the Magdalen, also in this room.

Justus Sustermans

Justus Sustermans (Antwerp, 1597-Florence, 1681), Portrait of Waldemar Christian, Prince of Denmark (oil on canvas, 70 × 54 cm.). The Flemish artist became the official portrait painter at the Medici court in 1619; in this capacity he executed numerous works with the assistance of a large workshop. The Gallery and the State Rooms contain many of his finest works. In this half-length portrait of the Danish prince Sustermans is at his best, drawing his inspiration above all from Velàzquez. True to his Flemish origin in the minute description of the white lace collar and the splendid damascened armour, the artist gives a penetrating and vivid analysis of the youthful countenance.

Velàzquez

Diego Velàzquez (Seville, 1599 - Madrid, 1660), Philip IV on Horseback (oil on canvas, 126 × 93 cm.). This is one of the rare examples of seventeenth-century Spanish painting in Italy and one of the very few that can be attributed to the greatest Spanish painter of that century or, as is the case here, to his immediate circle. Stylistically this fine portrait of the Spanish king cannot be regarded as entirely authentic. In fact it was sent to Florence as a working model for a bronze equestrian statue to be executed by the sculptor Pietro Tacca. Nevertheless, the portrait of Philip IV on horseback is typical of Velàzquez' workshop: the figure of the sovereign astride a splendid sorrel horse is set against a roughly sketched landscape background and an intense blue sky streaked with clouds. The king's features are unfathomable and almost distant in expression. The free brushwork evokes with a few strokes the shining armour, the different materials of his accoutrements and the red silk scarf, and the highlights have a silvery tone typical of the great Spanish artist.

LIST OF PAINTINGS NOT REPRODUCED

The Education of Jupiter Room

This elegantly decorated and gracefully proportioned ceiling was painted by Luigi Catani (1762-1840). At the centre of the ceiling is the scene which gives the room its name showing Jupiter reared and fed by nymphs and satyrs with the milk of the goat Amalthea. In the four lateral scenes are the Four Elements personified by Neptune and Amphitrite (Water), Juno (Air), Vulcan (Fire), and Cybele (Earth).

Caravaggio

Michelangelo Merisi, called Caravaggio (Caravaggio, 1573-Port' Ercole, 1610), Sleeping Cupid (oil on canvas, 72 × 105 cm.). The fame of this painting is shown by Giovanni da S. Giovanni's copy in the fresco decoration of a palace façade in Piazza S. Croce of around 1618. The painting dates from the period of Caravaggio's stay in Malta, probably 1608, only two years before his tragic death. Although a minor and small scale work it summarizes all the most typical aspects of the artist's mature style. The intense light, falling on the child's body, relaxed in sleep, underlines the forms with a strong sense of realism, accentuated by the use of an artificial source of light on the left, and transforms his features into a sort of grotesque mask. There is nothing charming about this sleeping urchin; only his wings barely visible in shadow and the quiver and arrows in the foreground tell us that the painting is more than simply the portrait of a naked child, asleep in a sultry Mediterranean night.

Cristofano Allori

Cristofano Allori (Florence, 1577-1621), Judith with the Head of Holofernes, detail (oil on canvas, 139 × 116 cm.). This splendid painting has been a famous and much admired object of study for generations and an illustrious example of a whole Florentine tradition of drawing. This work, although painted in the seventeenth century, still preserves sixteenth-century characteristics in the composition, in the range of colours which seem to be inspired by the Venetian school and in the purity of the drawing. Nevertheless, the attention given to the texture of the materials is new, as is also the use of dense pigment, not applied in varnishes but thick and rich.

Francesco Salviati

Francesco Salviati (Florence, 1510 - Rome, 1563), The Entombment (oil on panel, 55 × 77 cm.). This is a scene of intens pathos and is unusually dramatic for this elegant representativ of Tusco-Roman Mannerism, who also painted the splendi frescoes in one of the rooms of Palazzo Vecchio. Certain detail such as the heads in the foreground, betray the influence of Va sari, whereas others, for instance the figures in the right back ground, already reveal the artist's extremely personal style This painting may be the « modello » for an altarpiece of th same subject painted for the church of Corpus Domini in Ve nice in 1539-40.

LIST OF PAINTINGS NOT REPRODUCED

Barocci, F., *Portrait of Francesco Maria della Rovere*. Bilivert, G., *St. Sebastian*. Bonifacio de' Pitati, *Rest on the Flight to Egypt*. Bronzino, *Portrait o* *Don Garzia de' Medici; Portrait of Lucrezia de' Medici*. Crespi, G. M., *Portrait of an Old Man*. Dolci, C., *St. Andrew before the Cross; St. Carlo Bor* *romeo; St. Dominic in Penance; St. Nicholas of Tolentino*. Dyck, A. van, *Portrait of a Gentleman*. Dyck, A. van, (manner of), *Portrait of Henrietta of France* Filippo Napoletano, *The Man with the Snails*. Guercino, *Susannah and the Elders*. Mancini, B., *St. Cunegond and St. Henry; St. Francis Xavier*. Pietro da Cortona, *Death of St. Mary the Egyptian*. Ravesteyn, J. A. van, *Portrait of Daniel Heinsius*. Sustermans, J., *Holy Family; St. Sebastian; Head of the* *Virgin*. Veronese School, 16th century, *Portrait of a Sculptor*. Tintoretto, (school of), *Deposition*. Veronese, (school of), *Christ takes his leave from Mary* *before the Passion; The Marys at the Sepulchre; Resurrection*. Vicentino, A., *Herod's Feast*.

Sala della Stufa

The name of this room derives from the fact that it was previously a bathroom. It is famous for its fresco decoration, one of Pietro da Cortona's masterpieces. The walls are painted with scenes representing the Four Ages of Man (Gold, Silver, Copper and Iron) dating from between 1637 and 1640. The ceiling frescoes (Fame and the Four Cardinal Virtues) and those of the eight lunettes (allegorical figures of rulers) are by the Florentine Matteo Rosselli (1622), and the maiolica floor tiles (considerably restored) are by Benedetto Bocchi.

The Ulysses Room

The ceiling frescoes are by Gaspare Martellini (1785-1857) and represent Ulysses' home coming.

Raphael

Raphael, Madonna of the Impannata (oil on panel, 160 × 126 cm.). A mature work in which the more complex motifs contained in paintings such as the Madonna of the Chair are developed and extended to a large number of figures. The colour, too, has the richness of his later works and tends towards a blending of tones which he was to elaborate still further in the unfinished Transfiguration in the Vatican Museum. The painting derives its name from the «impannata» (a paper or cloth paned window) in the background.

Filippino Lippi

Filippino Lippi (Prato, 1457-1505), The Death of Lucretia (tempera on panel, 42 × 126 cm.). This painting, together with its pendant now in the Louvre, formed part of a cassone, the typical Florentine wedding chest in which the bride placed her dowry. Filippino, the son of Fra Filippo (see the tondo in the Prometheus Room), developed his style in the wake of a great pupil of his father's, Sandro Botticelli. He adopted the rhythmic quality of Botticelli's compositions, especially in his early period to which this painting belongs, portraying mythical or sacred subjects with animated and elegant lines and sober contrasts of bright colours against the light backgrounds of Renaissance buildings.

LIST OF PAINTINGS NOT REPRODUCED

Allori, C., *Portrait of a young Man; Portrait of a Man; St. John in the Wilderness.* Anonymous, 17th century, *Portrait of a Man.* Bassano, J. (School of), *Portrait of a Man.* Carracci, Ag., *Landscape.* Carracci, An., *Nymph and Satyr.* Campi, G., *Portrait of a Man.* Carpi, G. da, *Portrait of Alfonso d'Este.* Ciafferi, P., *Ecce Homo.* Cigoli, *Supper at Emmaus; Ecce Homo.* Correggio (copy), *Head of Christ.* Curradi, F., *St. Catherine.* Dolci, D., *Ecce Homo; Madonna and Child; Portrait of Claudia Felicita, wife of Leopold of Austria, with the attributes of Placidia; St. John on Patmos.* Dolci (School of), *St. Lucy.* Florentine School, 16th century, *Portrait of a Man.* Furini, F., *Allegorical Figure.* Moro, A. (School of), *Portrait of a Woman.* Moroni, G. B. (School of), *Portrait of Man with Beard; Portrait of a Man; Portrait of Bishop Girolamo Argentino.* Pagani, G., *Portrait of young Man, possibly of the Carafa Family.* Pourbus, F. the Younger, *Portrait of a Man.* Puligo, D., *Holy Family.* Reni, G., *Charity.* Riminaldi, O., *Cupid.* Rosa, S., *Temptations of St. Antony.* Sarto, A. del, *Madonna and Child with six Saints.* Schedoni, B., *St. Paul.* Schiavone, A., *Portrait of a Man in Franciscan Habit.* Tassi, A., *Diana and Acteon.* Tintoretto, J., *Portrait of Andrea Frizier.* Vasari G., *Temptation of St. Jerome.* Venetian School, 16th century, *Portrait of a Man.* Veronese School, 16th century, *Portrait of a Man.*

The Prometheus Room

The ceiling of this room was
frescoed by Giuseppe Collignon
(Siena, 1776-1863) with scenes

from the myth of Prometheus,
said to have brought fire and light
to mankind.

Filippo Lippi

Filippo Lippi (Florence, c. 1406 - Spoleto, 1469), Madonna and Child (tempera on circular panel, diam. 135 cm.). This tondo was painted around the mid-fifteenth century for the Bartolini family. The group of the Madonna and Child is not set against a neutral background or landscape but an interior in which a domestic scene is taking place. For the first time in Florentine art the iconography of the Madonna and Child acquires a new dimension which replaces its icon-like character with that of a genre scene. The use of the tondo, which here assumes a monumental scale, was also to become typical of Florentine art in the second half of the Quattrocento. The innovations of Lippi's art are visible in the geometrical perspective of the interior illuminated by a natural light, and in the small figures moving to an almost dance-like rhythm with an elegance which was to be of fundamental importance for his greatest pupil, Sandro Botticelli.

Botticelli

Alessandro Filipepi, called Sandro Botticelli (Florence, c. 1445-1510), Portrait of a Young Man wearing a « Mazzocchio » (oil on panel, 51 × 34 cm.). The bright red dress contrasting with the black « mazzocchio » (the typical Florentine hat worn in the Quattrocento) characterizes this portrait of a young man seen in a three-quarter pose typical of Botticelli. The artist always aims at giving his figures a sense of movement, almost of rotation, which results in an impression of restlessness even, as here, when the figure is actually static.

Botticelli

Alessandro Filipepi, called Sandro Botticelli, Portrait of a Woman, known as the Beautiful Simonetta (oil on panel, 61 × 4 cm.). The identification of this young woman as Simonetta Vespucci, the mistress of Giuliano de' Medici, is uncertain. The profile portrait still follows the iconographical pattern established by Domenico Veneziano, Baldovinetti and Pollaiolo in a series of well-known female portraits: the almost geometrical outline, the sobriety of the pale colours and the gentle melancholy of the sitter's expression nevertheless point to a difference in spirit and a new approach found throughout Botticelli's work.

Francesco Botticini

Francesco Botticini (Florence, 1446-1497), Madonna and Angels adoring the Christ Child (oil on circular panel, diam. 123 cm.). This tondo, in which the brilliant and perfectly preserved painting has been brought to light by a recent cleaning, was attributed in the past to Botticelli. Although influenced by the latter (especially in the graceful figures of the angels), this charming painting is certainly by Botticini. In the background is an extensive landscape with pointed hills and castles rendered in a range of blues. These and other details of the painting, such as the lizards, birds and minutely described leaves and flowers, show that Botticini was deeply influenced by contemporary Flemish painting.

Luca Signorelli

Luca Signorelli (Cortona, c. 1441-1523), The Holy Family (oil on circular panel, diam. 99 cm.). The emphasis on form characteristic of Signorelli's style is also present in this mature work. The figures, forming a compact group in the foreground, are boldly drawn to bring out the volumes which are further accentuated by the chiaroscuro so that they give the impression of being carved in stone.

Baldassare Peruzzi

Baldassarre Peruzzi (Siena, 1481 - Rome, 1536), Apollo Dancing with the Muses (oil on panel, 35 × 78.5 cm.). Formerly attributed to Giulio Romano, this small painting is, in fact, by another of Raphael's pupils, Baldassarre Peruzzi of Siena. The provenance of this painting is unknown; it is rather unusual both for its format and for its subject matter. The recent cleaning has revealed its intense colouring and the refined draughtsmanship of the figures, while their draperies give great vitality to the composition.

Bachiacca

Francesco Ubertini, called Bachiacca (Florence, 1494–1557), The Magdalen (oil on panel, 42 × 51 cm.). Of the same generation as Pontormo, Bachiacca was also an interpreter of Mannerism, that is to say of the refined and strongly intellectual style which developed in Florence as a conclusion to the Renaissance. Unlike Pontormo, Bachiacca did not take Michelangelo as his model, but found inspiration in Northern painting: this is evident in the almost enamelled finish of this work, in which the wax-like image of the saint with her shimmering red dress stands out against the compact green ground.

Guido Reni

Guido Reni (Bologna, 1575-1642), The Infant Bacchus (oil on canvas, 87 × 70 cm.). This is a well-known painting in which the luminous quality of the colours typical of Reni is combined with ample forms, still reminiscent of the style of his teacher, Annibale Carracci.

Pontormo

Jacopo Carrucci, called Pontormo (Pontormo, 1494 - Florence, 1556). The Martyrdom of the Theban Legion or Martyrdom of the Eleven Thousand (oil on panel, 67 × 73 cm.). Pontormo « painted..., in an infinite number of small figures, the story of eleven thousand martyrs condemned to death by Diocletian and all crucified in a wood; in it Jacopo represented a battle with horses and nude figures which is very fine; and several beautiful putti flying in the sky shooting arrows at the executioners. Also, around the emperor condemning them are several nudes going to their death, which are most beautiful » (Vasari). In this painting Pontormo gives an extremely personal and mannered interpretation of Michelangelo's art, which he admired and adopted as his canon of inspiration.

The Corridor of the Columns

This passage derives its name from the two oriental alabaster

columns flanking one of the doors.

Cornelis van Poelenburgh

Cornelis van Poelenburgh (Utrecht, c. 1586-1667). Landscape with Roman Ruins (oil on oval copper, 16 × 22 cm.). Poelenburgh, represented at the Pitti and the Uffizi by some of his finest works, spent about five years in Italy during which he paid a short visit to Florence. His interpretation of the Roman scene is more modern and realistic than that of Bril, by virtue of his sensitive interpretation and evocation of the limpid colours peculiar to Rome.

LIST OF PAINTINGS NOT REPRODUCED

Aelst, W. van., *Still Life with Birds*. Agricola, C. L., *Sunset Landscape; Landscape with Rainbow*. Boudewyns, A. F., *Landscape*. Bredael, J., *Landscape; Landscape*. Breenbergh, B., *Christ and the Adultress*. Brill, P., *Seascape; Mountainous Landscape; Landscape with Deer Hunt*. Brueghel, J., *Landscape*. Brueghel, P. the Younger, *Orpheus in the Underworld*. Douven, J. F., *Anna Maria Luisa de' Medici, Electress Palatine; The Electress Palatine in hunting dress; The Electress Palatine; The Elector and Electress Palatine dancing; The Elector and Electress Palatine*. Elsheimer, A. (attributed), *St. John the Baptist preaching*. Everdingen, A. van, *Landscape*. Francken, F. the Elder, *Allegory of Genius*. Francken, F. the Younger, *Triumph of Neptune and Amphitrite*. Kessel, J. van, *Still Life of Fruit and Fish; Studio of a Naturalist*. Molyn, P., *Landscape*. Momper, J. de, *Landscape with Ruins and Herdsmen*. Neer, E. van der, *Landscape; Landscape*. Poelenburgh, C. van, *Landscape with Figures Bathing; Finding of Moses; Roman Ruins; Landscape with two Peasants; Landscape with Ruined Castle; Moses striking the Rock; Five Saints; Ruins; Adoration of the Shepherds; Satyrs Dancing; Saints and Biblical Scenes; Landscapes with two Peasants and a Fountain; Landscape at Dusk; View of Roman Campagna; Ruins of the Palatine; Two small Landscapes* (Apparition of an Angel; Grotto); *Landscape with Shepherds Dancing*. Poelenburgh, C. van (School of), *Landscape with Nymphs and Satyrs Dancing*. Ryckaert, D., *Temptation of St. Anthony; Temptation of St. Anthony*. Schoevaerds, M., *Landscape*. Tassi, A. (attributed), *Venus and Cupid*. Teniers, D. the Elder, *Alchemist*. Vroom, H. C., *Seascape with Man-of-War*. Wittel, C. van, *Villa Medici in Rome; View of Rome; Castel Sant'Angelo; Roman View*. Wittenbroeck, M. van, *Roman Landscape*.

53

The Room of Justice

This room is named after the figure of Justice painted on the ceiling by Antonio Fedi (Florence, 1771-1843).

Titian

Titian, The Redeemer (oil on panel, 77 × 57 cm.). This picture was probably painted by Titian for Francesco Maria della Rovere, Duke of Urbino, in 1533-34. Like the Magdalen, it is on panel, which is unusual for Titian but more easily found in works dating from his early years. The style still reveals a pronounced interest in drawing and deep bright colours. A beautiful landscape forms the background to the majestic figure of Christ.

Veronese

Paolo Caliari, called Veronese, The Baptism of Christ (oil on canvas, 196.5 × 133 cm.). This painting suffered when it was enlarged in the seventeenth century, and also heavily restored. Nevertheless, the quality of the painting is discernible despite the former damages and varnishings. Brilliant in colour with subtle effects of light, the composition is conceived as an oval formed by the typically unbalanced figures against a beautiful landscape background.

Titian

Titian, Portrait of Vincenzo Mosti (oil on canvas, 85 × 66 cm.). This portrait, partly because of an inscription on the reverse, was believed to represent Vincenzo's brother, Tommaso. Vincenzo Mosti, the Ferrarese man of letters, was an intimate friend of Duke Alfonso d'Este, and Titian painted his portrait in Ferrara in 1526. In this portrait the Venetian artist already reveals the considerable skill which was to reach its full development in works such as the portrait of Aretino (The Venus Room). As for The Man with Grey Eyes, Titian again uses Mosti's dress to create a series of tonal variations of black against black, animated by the fur visible through the slashes of his sleeves and a play of whites in the pleated shirt collar, enhanced by a thin black border.

Giovan Battista Moroni

Giovan Battista Moroni (Bergamo, c. 1525-1578), Portrait of a Woman (oil on canvas, 53 × 45.5 cm.). Moroni belongs to the rich Venetian culture of the « terra ferma » which is characterized, figuratively, by a realistic contact with life evident in this fine female portrait (and also in two other portraits by the artist at the Pitti) in which the features and personality of the sitter are sharply but sensitively rendered without any attempt at idealization which would have betrayed her slightly provincial awkwardness. Particularly remarkable is the chromatic subtlety in the treatment of the dress and hair.

LIST OF PAINTINGS NOT REPRODUCED

Bassano, J., *Portrait of a Woman*. Bassano, L., *Last Supper*. Bonifacio Veronese, *Finding of Moses; Rest on the Flight into Egypt; Portrait of a Woman; Augustus and the Sibyl*. Garofalo, *St. James the Great*. Moroni, G. B., *Portrait of a Man*. Tintoretto, J., *Madonna and Child; Portrait of a young Man; Portrait of an old Man in Red; Portrait of a Man*. Titian (School of), *Portrait of a Man*. Venetian School, 16th century, *Portrait of Costanza Bentivoglio; Portrait of a Man; Holy Family with St. Elizabeth*. Veronese, P., *Portrait of a Man*.

The Flora Room

The fresco after which this small room is named is by Antonio Marini (Prato, 1788-1861).

Canova

Antonio Canova (Possagno, 1757 - Venice, 1822), *Venus*, Carrara marble, height 170 cm). This statue was carved by Canova for Napoleon in 1810: it was intended to replace the famous Medici Venus removed from the Tribuna of the Uffizi and taken to Paris with many other works of art from Florence in 1799 (given back after 1815). Canova's virtuosity in the working of marble is supreme; the material becomes transparent and luminous and is transformed by the artist through the different degrees of polishing to render a variety of textures: the softly-bound hair, the transparent skin of her perfect body, the greater weight of the drapery with which the goddess, after her bath, modestly covers herself. The desire to emulate models of classical antiquity and to rival their perfection does not diminish the deeply personal quality which makes this statue a masterpiece.

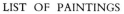

LIST OF PAINTINGS
Allori, A., *Madonna and Child; St. John the Baptist Preaching*. Bronzino, *Portrait of Laudomia de' Medici; Portrait of Luca Martini*. Cigoli, *Portrait o' a Man*. Gennari, B., *David*. Ghirlandaio, M. di R. del, *Holy Family with St. John; Portrait of a Woman with a white Veil*. Piombo, S. del, *Martyrdom of St. Agatha*. Pontormo, *Adoration of the Magi*. Puligo, D., *Madonna and Child with infant St. John; Portrait of Piero Carnesecchi; Madonna and Child with Saints; St. Mary Magdalen*. Sarto, A. del, *Two Scenes from the Story of Joseph*.

The Putti Room

The fresco on the ceiling of this room is also by Antonio Marini (1788-1861).

Godfried Schalken

Godfried Schalken (Made, 1643 - The Hague, 1706), Girl Holding a Candle (oil on canvas, 61 × 50 cm.). Schalken was a pupil of the famous Gerhard Honthorst, who invented the theme of figures seen by candlelight, and was fond of this type of scene. The Girl Holding a Candle is one of Schalken's best known works and one which comes closest to those of his teacher.

Rubens

Peter Paul Rubens. The Three Graces (oil on canvas, 47 × 36 cm.). Here Rubens used a technique known as grisaille painting (monochrome with grey as the basic colour and white highlights). Despite this technique which was then fairly common (see van Dyck's Madonna in Glory in the Corridor of the Columns), Rubens succeeds in giving luminosity to the female nudes. The master's touch gives movement and life to the composition with an immediacy and freedom typical of his oil sketches.
Rubens frequently made use of this technique, but usually in preparatory sketches for larger works. These small panels, executed with incredible brio and speed, represent the artist's first ideas. However, in the case of the Three Graces no larger scale version of the same composition is known.

Karl Andreas Ruthart

Karl Andreas Ruthart (Danzig, c. 1630 - Aquila, c. 1703), Wild Animals, detail (oil on canvas, 104 × 142 cm.). Ruthart specialized in painting animals. This painting, with its pendant of Tigers Attacking a Stag, illustrates another genre typical of Northern art in the seventeenth and eighteenth centuries: scenes with animals, which were to have an extensive influence on French Romantic painting.

Willem van Aelst

Willem van Aelst (Delft, 1626-c. 1683), Still Life with Game (oil on canvas, 1.25 × 0.99 cm.). Van Aelst enjoyed a considerable reputation at the Medici court where he spent a few years and left some of his finest still-life paintings (see this room and the Fame Room). Skilled in this typically Dutch genre, the artist achieved effects of great subtlety in the representation of objects and natural forms with a masterly technique and refined choice of colour.

Rachel Ruysch

Rachel Ruysch (Amsterdam, 1664–1750), Flowers, Fruits and Insects (oil on canvas, 89 × 69 cm.). The painting is signed on the left and dated 1716. Ruysch was a pupil of Otto Marseus van Schrieck (see The Fame Room), a specialist in still-life painting who combined the representation of natural flora with that of small animals insects and reptiles. Rachel Ruysch became famous for her spectacular compositions of plants, flowers and fruits.

Ludolf Backhuysen

Ludolf Backhuysen (Emden, 1631 - Amsterdam, 1708). Boats in a Rough Sea (oil on canvas, 65 × 79 cm.). Backhuysen belongs to the current of Dutch landscape painters of the seventeenth century who carried the observation of nature to an amazing degree of refinement. A late follower in the marine genre (with Dubbels, represented in the same room), the artist shows considerable skill in his rendering of the grey tones of the sea and sky in a storm.

LIST OF PAINTINGS NOT REPRODUCED
Aelst, W. van, *Fruit; Kitchen Still Life; Still Life with Flowers*. Brill, P., *Landscape with Figures and Cattle; Landscape with Herdsman*. Cerquozzi, M., *Linen Carder; Herdsman with Dog*. Dubbels, H. J., *Seascape*. Galle, G., *Festoon of Flowers*. Hondius, A., *Boar Hunt*. Jordaens, J., *Neptune creating the Horse*. Laer, P. van, *Country Stable*. Mieris, W. van, *St. Mary Magdalen*. Mignard, P., *Portrait of the Marquise de Sevigné*. Ruthart, C. A., *Tigers attacking a Stag*. Ruysch, R., *Fruit and Flowers*. Swanevelt, H. van, *Landscape*.

The Poccetti Gallery

This small gallery which was built during the reign of Cosimo II de' Medici (1609-1621), was frescoed with allegorical subjects in the years 1625-1630 by Matteo Rosselli and his followers. The decoration of the lower part of the wall dates from 1813 when. the adjacent Loggia was closed.

Gaspard Dughet

Gaspard Dughet (Rome, 1615-1675), Landscape with Dancing Fauns (oil on canvas, 51 × 87 cm.). This and the three other landscapes exhibited in this room form a series depicting some of the most evocative spots of the Roman Campagna (Tivoli) and the immediate surroundings of Rome (St. Peter's and the Tiber valley). Their limpid colouring echoes the classicism of Dughet's famous brother-in-law, Nicolas Poussin, who initiated Dughet in the art of painting. These four examples of Dughet's late style give an idea of his interesting personality, which not only had a considerable influence on artists of his day but continued into the eighteenth and early nineteenth centuries.

Domenico Feti

Domenico Feti (Rome, c. 1589 - Venice, 1624), The Labourers in the Vineyard, detail (oil on panel, 75.8 × 44.5 cm.). This small painting, striking for its rich and brilliant colouring, is the companion to another parable scene, The Lost Groat, in the same gallery, which also contains a third painting by Feti of St. Margaret of Cortona Overcoming the Devil.

Rubens

Peter Paul Rubens, Portrait of George Villiers, First Duke of Buckingham (oil on panel, 65 × 50 cm.). George Villiers (1592-1628), favourite of Charles I, was created Duke of Buckingham and Prime Minister. However, the Duke lost the support of Parliament and was a bad adviser to the King. He was assassinated by a fanatic while still in his prime. The Duke posed for Rubens in Paris and this painting was based on the sketch from life. Its pendant is the portrait reputed to be of Catherine Manners, Duchess of Buckingham.

The Music Room and the Castagnoli Room

The Music Room

This fine room, whose brightness is enhanced by the colour of the cipolin marble columns, is a particularly impressive example of Neo-classical taste: the ceiling is decorated with frescoes by Luigi Ademollo (Milan, 1764-1849) simulating a frieze in relief commemorating the liberation of Vienna from the Turks (1683), and a central allegory of the glories of the Imperial House of the Hapsburgs. In the centre of the room, beneath a superb chandelier of crystal and gilded bronze, is an ormolu table by Pierre Philippe Thomire (dated 1819) with a top of Russian malachite. The drums lining the walls are among the finest pieces of Neoclassical furniture produced in Florence in the nineteenth century.

The Castagnoli Room

This room, dominated by two colossal marble sculptures of a Prisoner and Augustus (restored copies after the original), derives its name from Giuseppe Castagnoli (1754-1832) who executed the decoration of painted trompe-l'oeil architecture and sculptures (in the lunettes, busts of Pietro Leopoldo and Ferdinand III of Lorraine; ceiling tondo, Chariot of the Sun). In the centre of the room is one of the most famous works produced by the Opificio delle Pietre Dure (The Pietra Dura Workshop), which was founded by the Medici and flourished under the Lorraine, as is shown by the many splendid tables in the Gallery, the Museo degli Argenti (The Medici Treasures) and the State Apartments. The table is known as the Table of the Muses at the centre is Apollo's chariot surrounded by symbols of the Arts in inlaid hardstones and semiprecious stones set in lapis lazuli, producing a brilliant effect of colour (the top was begun in the early nineteenth century but only completed in 1822); the bronze base is by the sculptor Giovanni Dupré (Siena, 1817-1882).

The Room of Allegory

This is the first room of the wing named after Volterrano (Baldassarre Franceschini), the artist responsible for the decoration. The ceiling frescoes framed by the white and gold stucco decoration, clearly inspired by the great ceilings by Pietro da Cortona in the State Rooms, represen allegories alluding to the name of Vittoria della Rovere who live in this part of the palace.

Francesco Furini

Francesco Furini (Florence, 1603-1646), Faith (oil on canvas, 65 × 49.5 cm.). This delicate figure is typical of the painter who was one of the most distinguished artistic personalities in Florence in the first half of the seventeenth century (there are frescoes by him in the Room of Giovanni da S. Giovanni in the Museo degli Argenti). Furini is particularly famous for his luminous female nudes (see Hylas and the Nymphs in the Bernice Room in this wing), characterized by a soft sensuality. Also typical of the artist is his use of soft chiaroscuro in half-light which accentuates the pre-Romantic character of his painting.

Volterrano

Baldassarre Franceschini, called Volterrano, Venal Love (fresco 64 × 45 cm.). This painting and the Sleeping Love are among the artist's most typical works. The graceful figure, rich i subtle humour, of a young woman laughing mischievousl; forms the subject of this allegory. The light, rapid techniqu heralds an almost eighteenth-century decorative elegance.

Volterrano

Baldassarre Franceschini, called Volterrano (Volterra, 1611 - Florence, 1689), A Trick of the Pievano Arlotto (tempera on canvas, 107 × 150 cm). Volterrano was fond of a clear linear style of painting; here he employed a thin tempera medium instead of oil paint, which accounts for the freshness of colours similar to that produced by fresco technique. Arlotto was a parson who lived in the fifteenth century and became a legendary figure as a result of his practical jokes. Volterrano, who also painted an imaginary portrait of the Pievano exhibited nearby, chose to depict one of his most celebrated tricks. Here is a vivid, unconventional scene of a merry party portrayed with a sharp sense of humour which brings to mind a whole tradition of Florentine literature.

LIST OF PAINTINGS NOT REPRODUCED

Allori, C., *Infant Christ Asleep; St. Mary Magdalen in the Desert; Madonna and Child*. Altissimo, C. dell'. *Portrait of Clarice Ridolfi Altoviti*. Bronzino (School of), *Portrait of Cosimo I de' Medici; Portrait of a Woman; Portrait of a Woman*. Florentine School, 16th century, *Portrait of a Woman; Venus and Adonis*. Fontana, L., *Pourtrait of a Woman of the Ruini Family*. Fontebuoni, A., *St. John the Baptist in the Wilderness*. Gentileschi, A., *Madonna and Child*. Giovanni di San Giovanni, *Christ in the Desert; Painting; The Pievano Arlotto; Mystic Marriage of St. Catherine; Venus combing Cupid's Hair*. Luti, B., *Cherub's Head; Head of young Girl*. Marinari, O., *David*. Maso da San Fiano, *Portrait of Elena Gaddi Quaratesi*. Mehus, L., *Assumption of the Magdalen; Magdalen Asleep*. Pagani, G., *Tobias curing his Father*. Pourbus, F. the Younger, *Portrait of Elizabeth of France, Queen of Spain, as a Child; Portrait of Louis XIII as a boy*. Procaccini, G., *Nativity*. Sustermans, J., *Portrait of Maximilian III, Archduke of Austria; Portrait of a Man; Portrait of Cosimo III de' Medici; Portrait of Margherita de' Medici, wife of Odoardo I of Parma; Portrait of Puliciani; Portrait of Caterina Puliciani*. Volterrano, *Cupid Asleep; Portrait of an Augustinian; Portrait of Antonio Baldinucci; Portrait of an Algerian Bey*.

The Fine Arts Room and other Rooms

The Fine Arts Room

The ceiling is by Domenico Podestà (d. 1862) and represents Jupiter sending Iris and Minerva to introduce the Arts to mankind, personified by allegorical figures of Painting, Sculpture and Architecture.

Emilio Zocchi

Emilio Zocchi (Florence, 1835-1913), Young Michelangelo Carving a Faun's Head (height 60 cm.). The sculpture is signed and dated 1861. It illustrates an episode from Michelangelo's beginnings as an artist when, still a child, he was discovered by Lorenzo the Magnificent who put him to study under Bertoldo, the pupil of Donatello, in the garden of S. Marco. The sculpture is kept in the Room of the Allegory.

LIST OF PAINTINGS
Allori, C., *Adoration of the Magi.* Anonymous, 17th century, *Portrait of a Woman.* Barocci, F., *Head of an Angel; Head of the Virgin of the Annunciation.* Cigoli, *Deposition; Madonna and Child with Book; Martyrdom of St. Stephen; St. Francis in Adoration; Stigmatization of St. Francis.* Dolci, C., *Madonna appearing to St. Louis of Toulouse.* Florentine School, 16th century, *Portrait of a Woman.* Manetti, R., *Death of St. Mary Magdalen.* Raphael (School of), *Holy Family.* Salviati, F., *Portrait of a Man.* Vignali, J., *Baptism of Constantine.*

The Aurora Room

The ceiling frescoes by Gaspare Martellini (Florence, 1785-1857) illustrate the theme after which the room is named: the figure of Aurora mounted on Pegasus is surrounded by various allegorical figures of the Arts and Time. Above the cornice is a bust of Ferdinand III of Lorraine, the Grand Duke who commissioned many of the interior decorations of the palace after his return to Florence in 1815.

LIST OF PAINTINGS
Boscoli, A., *Birth of the Virgin.* Empoli, *St. Ivo and his Pupils; The Drunkenness of Noah.* Flemish School, 17th century, *St. Jerome.* Fontana, L., *Portrait of Francesco Panigarola, the Milanese Preacher.* Ligozzi, J., *Adoration of the Magi.* Lippi, L., *Jacob at the Well; Triumph of David.* Sustermans, J., *Portrait of Prince Czomodanoff, Ambassador of Moscow.* Vasari, G., *Birth of the Virgin; Vison of Count Hugo.*

The Hercules Room

Pietro Benvenuti (Arezzo, 1769-1844) painted the frescoes illustrating the legend of Hercules on the walls of this room designed and decorated by the architect Giuseppe Cacialli (Florence, 1770-1828). Both artists are among the major figures of Tuscan Neoclassicism and the Hercules Room is certainly one of the most successful creations in this style. Exceptionally fine are the two tables with porphyry tops decorated with pietra-dura inlays and the large Sèvres porcelain vase mounted in gilded bronze, the latter by Pierre Philippe Thomire (Paris, 1751-1843), who also made the malachite table in the Music Room.

The Bernice Room

Giuseppe Bezzuoli (Florence 1784-1855), one of the most important Tuscan painters of the early nineteenth century, painted the ceiling fresco, representing Titus leaving Bernice, and the four lunettes with the Cardinal Virtues.

LIST OF PAINTINGS

Albani, F., *Liberation of St. Peter*. Allori, C., *St. Mary Magdalen; Adoration of the Magi; Tobias and the Angel*. Bilivert, G., *Joseph and Potiphar's Wife*. Curradi, F., *Narcissus*. Dolci, C., *Agony in the Garden; St. Simon*. Filippo Napoletano, *Landscape; Landscape*. Furini, F., *Adam and Eve*. Rimi-naldi, O., *Martyrdom of St. Cecilia*.

The Psyche Room

The nineteenth-century decoration, with the rape of Psyche at the centre of the ceiling, was painted by Giuseppe Collignon (Siena, 1776-1863).

LIST OF PAINTINGS

Rosa S., *Uprooted Tree and Seated Man; Tree and Man in Profile; Battle Scene; Empedocles throwing himself into the Crater; Seascape with Tower; Landscape with natural Arch; Landscape with Figures; Landscape with an Oriental; Landscape with two Men; Philosophers in a Wood*.

The Fame Room

The ceiling is decorated with allegorical scenes by an unidentified artist active in the third or fourth decade of the nineteenth century. From this room one passes through the circular vestibule, containing statues of Venus and Mercury and a central vase with alabaster handles, to the beautiful bathroom of Marie Louise of Bourbon, Queen of Etruria, built by Cacialli around 1806.

LIST OF PAINTINGS

Aelst, W. van, *Musical Instruments, Fruit, Arms and Game; Vase of Flowers and a Clock; Still Life with Melon*. Brueghel, J., *Madonna and Child in a Garland of Flowers*. Calvaert, D., *Assumption of the Virgin*. Clouet, F., *Portrait of Henry II of France*. Clouet, J., *Portrait of the Duc de Guise*. Dolci, C, *Repentant St. Peter*. Filippo Napoletano, *Crucifixion; A Mill; Landscape*. Floris, F., *Adam and Eve*. Key, T., *Portrait of a Man*. Marseus, O., *Plants, Flowers, Butterflies and Rodents; Plants and Butterflies; Plants, Butterflies and Reptiles*. Pillment, J. B., *Seascape; Shipwreck*. Pourbus, F. the Younger, *Orpheus playing to the Animals*. Sammacchini, O., *Holy Family*. Venetian School, 16th century, *Holy Family*. Wittel, G. van, *View of Posillipo; View of Verona; View of Naples; View of the Monastery of S. Paolo at Albano*.

* Positioning of paintings on October 30th, 1972, which may be altered.

Museo degli Argenti

The ground floor rooms, which were originally reserved for the reception of important visitors, in 1919 became the setting for the newly-founded Museo degli Argenti, composed of what remained of the treasures collected by the Medici and later by the Hapsburg-Lorraine rulers. The first three rooms were frescoed between 1638 and 1644 by A. M. Colonna and A. Mitelli with illusionistic architecture on the walls and with scenes of Jupiter descending from Olympus to give the Medici the insignia of power, Stories and the Triumph of Alexander and an Allegory of Strength, Justice and Time on the ceilings. From here one passes through a small chapel into the splendid Hall of the Argenti, decorated for the marriage of Ferdinand II de' Medici and Vittoria della Rovere from 1634 onwards with frescoes by Giovanni da San Giovanni (on the ceiling, The Wedding Celebrations; on the walls, Books destroyed by Time and Satyrs; Mahomet preparing to destroy Greek civilization; Satyrs invading Parnassus and Harpies driving out the Muses), Cecco Bravo (Lorenzo the Magnificent welcoming the Muses and Virtues), Ottavio Vannini (Lorenzo surrounded by Artists; Allegories of Faith and Prudence) and Francesco Furini (Lorenzo and the Platonic Academy at Careggi; Allegory of Lorenzo's death). The other rooms are decorated with tapestries of Florentine manufacture of the late sixteenth and seventeenth centuries.

The collection has two basic nuclei: the works of art commissioned by the Medici family from the fifteenth century onwards from local or foreign artists in Florence; and the precious group of works brought to Florence from abroad, chiefly from Germany and Austria, as a result of such marriages as that of Christina of Lorraine, or Anna Maria Luisa, the last of the Medici, to the Elector Palatine of Düsseldorf, and also by the Lorraine Dukes, in particular Ferdinand III after his return from exile following the Napoleonic interregnum. Besides these, there are objects which were acquired outside Italy including works in amber and ivory from Germany, and gifts to the Grand Dukes. The rarest and most precious pieces in the Museum are the antique vases from the collection of Lorenzo the Magnificent (exhibited in the Room of Giovanni da S. Giovanni), which were given silver-gilt mounts in the fifteenth century and later, and originally came from the Medici Palace in the Via Larga. These vases are of semi-precious stones and Lorenzo had them engraved with his initials (LAVR MED). Alongside these are other objects of early date and beautiful workmanship including goblets, drinking horns, cups of briar wood, coconut or ostrich eggs, splendidly mounted in gilded silver and enamel; also the

Room IV with frescoes by Giovanni da San Giovanni (1635-36), Francesco Furini, Cecco Bravo and Ottavio Vannini (1638-42)

Room II, frescoed by Agostino Mitelli and Angelo Michele Colonna (1638-44)

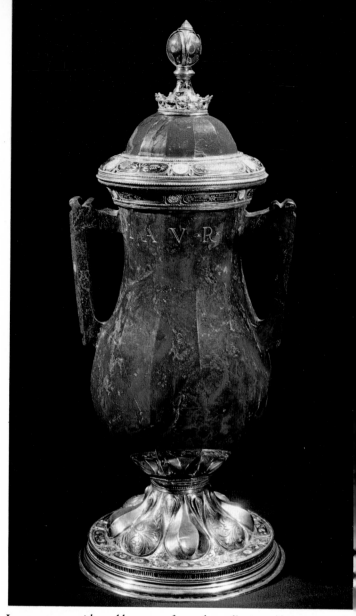

Lapis-lazuli vase by Bernardo Buontalenti with enamelled gold mount by Jacques Bilivert (1583)

Jasper vase with gold mount from the collection of Lorenzo the Magnificent, thirteenth-century Venetian work with enamelled silver mount by Giusto da Firenze (c. 1465)

Casket in rock crystal and gilt and enamelled silver by Valerio Belli of Vicenza (1532)

jewels and goldsmith works originally owned by the Prince Bishops of Salzburg and brought to Florence by Ferdinand III in 1815, which constitute a complex of exceptional artistic and historical interest. Some of the finest pieces in the Museum date from the sixteenth century. Among the finest Italian works of that period is the casket with scenes of Christ's Passion engraved in rock crystal, commissioned by Pope Clement VII de' Medici from Valerio Belli of Vicenza as a gift to Francis I of France on the occasion of the

Rock-crystal vase in the shape of a bird with enamelled gold mount, Florentine workmanship (c. 1580)

Pietra-dura mosaic outlined in gold representing the Signoria Square by Bernardino Gaffuri (1598)

marriage of his son Henry II to Catherine de' Medici; the famous lapis lazuli flask mounted in gold, enamels and precious stones by the Dutch goldsmith Jacques Bilivert, active at the Medici court, on a design by Bernardo Buontalenti (1583); the bird-shaped vase in rock crystal mounted in gold and enamels exquisitely engraved; the rock-crystal flask of Milanese workmanship engraved with scenes representing Parnassus; and the oval plaque in pietra-dura inlay outlined in gold with the Piazza della Signoria, a Florentine work of the end of the century. Among the non-Italian works of exceptional quality is the so-called Cup of Diane de Poitiers, a spectacular chalice in rock crystal with a gilded and enamelled cover, executed for Henry II of France, whose initials entwined with those of Diane or Catherine de' Medici (his wife) form the monogram incorporated in the splendid design of the lid; the Mexican mitre of feather-mosaic and gold with scenes of the Passion of around 1560; the holy-water vessel of 1577 from Augsburg; the series of fifty-four silver-gilt cups from Salzburg and the splendid dishes, ewers and basins from the same source. Together with the late sixteenth-century jewels of German craftsmanship they constitute an impressive and important group of Northern goldsmith's work.

The seventeenth and eighteenth centuries are represented mostly by works produced in the Grand-Ducal workshops in Florence, which developed as a result of the Medici's interest in the minor arts, and in which foreign craftsmen were also employed. Besides the already mentioned ivory vases (especially fine are those by Eisenberg and Sengher), there are also statuettes and reliefs in ivory by B. Stockamer, B. Permoser and others, executed with extreme skill and in a

73

Mosaic of pietra dura, precious stones and enamelled gold representing Cosimo II in prayer, made in the Grand Ducal Workshop (1617-24, with a late eighteenth-century frame)

Table top designed by Antonio Cioci in pietra dura inlaid in green marble, executed in the Grand Ducal Pietra-Dura Workshop, representing a still life of porcelain objects (1792)

Table top representing the port of Leghorn, executed in pietra-dura inlay by Cristofano Gaffuri after a drawing by Jacopo Ligozzi (1600-04)

Jewels in the form of sailing vessels in enamelled gold and precious stones, German goldsmith's work, late sixteenth century

style that reflects Baroque taste. Among the many works in precious stones and metals in the Museum we shall single out the relief in gold, enamels and precious stones of Cosimo II kneeling before an altar (with the Florentine cathedral and Giotto's tower in the background), executed by various artists working for the Medici; the German flasks and gold cups decorated with «grotesques» from Salzburg; the splendid vase in pure rock crystal with an enamelled gold mount set with emeralds and rubies by the French goldsmith Odoardo Vallet; the various reliquaries and curiosities

Perfume jar in ivory, gold and precious stones, Dresden manufacture of the early eighteenth century

Sèvres vase representing the Egyptian Expedition by Johann Jakob Swebach (1798)

Sèvres porcelain plaque with a portrait of Napoleon, by François-Pascal Simon after Gérard (early nineteenth century)

crowding the cases. Two large-scale objects, which cannot really be termed pieces of furniture, are the two cabinets in the Museum, of which there are others in the State Apartments: the so-called Stipo d'Alemagna (German Cabinet), made in Augsburg around 1625, of ebony with delicately painted panels in hardstone; the other, known as the Cabinet of the Elector Palatine, a gift of Cosimo III de' Medici to his son-in-law, the Elector Palatine of Düsseldorf, designed by G. B. Foggini, the greatest Florentine architect and sculptor of the late seventeenth and early eighteenth centuries. It is a typical and sumptuous example of Baroque taste, in which the ebony, gilded bronze, enamels and pietra-dura inlays together produce a striking effect.

Like the Palatine Gallery and the Museum of the Opificio delle Pietre Dure (Pietra Dura Workshop), the Museo degli Argenti is also extremely rich in tables with tops of semiprecious stones and pietra dura dating from the late sixteenth to the nineteenth centuries.

The Museum also comprises a large porcelain section, mostly of eighteenth and nineteenth-century non-Italian pieces, which are waiting to be displayed in the Villa del Cavaliere, high up in the Boboli Gardens. The major porcelain collections are those of Vincennes, Saxony and Sèvres, which often reached Florence as gifts from other ruling princes.

State Apartments

The State Apartments (formerly Royal Apartments) occupy the right-hand half of the first floor of the palace. Their appearance today is largely that given to them by the Lorraine Grand Dukes on their return to Florence after the fall of the Napoleonic Empire (1815), and many rooms are elegantly decorated with white and gold stucco work. The most outstanding room is the oval Queen's Dressing Room, which has partially coloured stuccoes and a pink marble mantle-piece. Most of the rooms were transformed in the Neoclassical period, except for the sixteenth-century Room of Bona and the Chapel which had been Prince Ferdinand de' Medici's bedroom (d. 1713) and still preserves its late seventeenth-century character. The State Apartments also contain a few but important pieces of furniture from the Medici period including two typical Florentine Baroque cabinets: one of ebony with inlays of pietra dura and gilded bronze, which belonged to the Grand Duchess Vittoria della Rovere; the other of ebony and ivory with ivory carvings. Other elegant examples of late-Baroque Florentine taste are the prie-dieu of ebony, bronze, pietra dura and semi-precious stones with a matching frame containing a Madonna by Carlo Dolci and a holywater stoup, designed by G. B. Foggini (1652-1737). Several rooms are hung with French tapestries which were brought to Florence from Parma: particularly fine is the series of Hunts of Louis XV based on cartoons by J. B. Oudry, court painter to the French king, and woven by Audran (who also executed those of the Story of Esther on drawings by De Troy). The furnishing of some rooms, including the Throne Room and the Red Sitting Room or King's Sitting Room, dates from the Savoy period, when Florence was the capital of Italy (1865-1871). There are paintings hanging in all the rooms, mostly portraits of historical figures, both of the Medici period (chiefly by Sustermans), and later.

Queen Margherita's Dressing Room by Ignazio Pellegrini (second half of the eighteenth century)

Sala Bianca (the White Room), architecture by Gaspare Maria Paoletti with stuccowork by Grato Albertolli (1776-80)

Room of the Niches, decorated by Giuseppe Maria Terreni and Giuseppe Castagnoli (late eighteenth century)

Room of Bona, frescoed by Bernardino Poccetti (1608)

Private alcove of Ferdinando de' Medici (1657–1713), perhaps designed by Giovanni Battista Foggini, and transformed into a chapel in the 18th century.

Ebony and ivory cabinet designed by Giovanni Battista Foggini (late seventeenth century)

Anna Maria Luisa's holy water stoup, designed by Giovanni Battista Foggini, made in the Grand Ducal Workshops (1704)

Portrait of Stanislao Poniatowski by Marcello Bacciarelli (end of the eighteenth century)

The Throne Room, showing the ceiling by Giuseppe Castagnoli (eighteenth century)

Tapestry from the series of « Hunts of Louis XV », of Gobelins manufacture, woven by Jean Audran on cartoons by Jean-Baptiste Oudry (1735-45)

Gallery of Modern Art

The third important art collection in the Pitti is the Gallery of Modern Art, founded towards 1860 but re-arranged at about the same time as the creation of the Museo degli Argenti owing to its removal to the Pitti from the Academy of Fine Arts after 1918. The collection is very large (about two thousand works) and provides, above all, a thorough documentation of the Tuscan school, whereas the other Italian schools are represented only very sparsely and unequally. The arrangement of the Gallery is conditioned by the rooms which date from the Lorraine period, when Ferdinand III and Leopold II transformed the top floor of the palace to house the Palatine Library, but which remained unfinished as a result of subsequent historical events. Nineteenth-century academism gives the Gallery its prevailing tone, represented by artists belonging to this trend of taste which was common to most of Europe from the late eighteenth century onwards. The first rooms contain works of the neoclassical period, mostly by Tuscan artists such as Pietro Benvenuti (Saxons swearing allegiance to Napoleon; Portrait of Countess Elena Mastiani Brunacci), Francesco Nenci (Oedipus rescued by the Shepherds), Giuseppe Bezzuoli (Entry of Charles VIII into Florence; Portrait of the Grand Duchess Maria Antonietta) and Stefano Tofanelli (Portrait of Francesco Belluomini). The sculptures of this period include works by Canova (Head of Napoleon) and Lorenzo Bartolini (Carlo Ludovico di Borbone, Duke of Lucca; Model for the Demidoff Monument). Next follows the section devoted to Romantic painting, headed by the Venetian Francesco Hayez (The two Foscari), and historical painting of the first half of the nineteenth century, which was the speciality of Tuscan artists uch as Luigi Sabatelli (Farinata degli Uberti at the battle of he Serchio), Francesco Sabatelli (Ajax clinging to the rock) und Enrico Pollastrini (The Flooding of the Serchio in 1840). Among the North Italian painters present are Piccio (Giovanni Battista Carnovali: Portrait of Signora Marini), the landscape painter Antonio Fontanesi (Landscape after a rain shower) and Massimo d'Azeglio (Arab cavalry), and genre painters such as Domenico Induno (The Antiquary). There is also a series of sculptural works ranging from the Tuscan sculptors Giovanni Dupré (Cain and Abel) and Pietro Tenerani (Psyche) to the Roman Odoardo Fantacchiotti (Susanna of 1870). The purists of the Tuscan school are also well represented: Luigi Mussini Eudorus and Cimodoce of 1855; Allegory of Music), Antonio Ciseri (group of drawings and sketches; portraits of Gino Capponi, Gaetano Bianchi, etc.; the famous Ecce Homo), Stefano Ussi (Expulsion of the Duke of Athens of 1860 - which received he first prize at the Universal Exhibition held in Paris in 1867) und Alcide Segoni (Discovery of Catiline's body).

n strong contrast to these works are those belonging to the ypically Tuscan, certainly more « modern » and revolutionary current in nineteenth-century Italy, known as the « Macchiaioli » movement. The development of this trend was virtually limited to Tuscany, apart from sporadic contacts (Signorini) with other Italian regions or with more advanced movements in Europe French Impressionism). The weak and rather solitary protest of the « Macchiaioli » against academic and historical painting took the form of rather small works directly inspired by nature, n which the images are built up by spots (macchie) of colour, hence the name Macchiaioli), and contrasts of light. Of the Macchiaioli, the most complex, if not the most important personality, Giovanni Fattori (1825-1908) practised a form of history painting but always interpreted his subjects in the light of a spontaneous « realism » drawing his inspiration from life to describe soldiers in action (Soldier falling from his mount; Cavalry charge of 1873) or the rapidly executed scenes of fighting and camping (Battle of Custoza of 1880; Italian camp after the Battle of Magenta of 1862). The Gallery is particularly rich n works by this painter, ranging from the complete collection of his etchings to landscapes and scenes of life in Maremma Shepherds with their flocks; Market in Maremma; the Oxcart; The Rotonda at Palmieri). More lyrical and poetic and

Giuseppe de Nittis (Barletta 1846 - Paris 1884), Beach near Barletta.

Antonio Canova (Possagno 1757 - Venice 1822), Head of Napoleon I, marble

Giovanni Fattori (Livorno 1825 - Florence 1908), Soldier Falling from his Mount

very different in character is Silvestro Lega (1826-1895), who interpreted landscape with greater subtlety and feeling, bathing his subjects in soft, grey-green tonalities (Bersaglieri leading Austrian prisoners). Another well documented figure is Telemaco Signorini (1835-1901) who, besides studying the simple formal contrasts of nature, painted small-scale views and interiors with scenes of everyday life (Garden at Careggi; Leith). Close in spirit to the Macchiaioli, but also linked to a more European culture, was Giovanni Boldini (1842-1931) of Ferrara, who is well represented by a series of rapid sketches, mostly portraits, which illustrate the artist's accomplished but superficial style (Portrait of Mrs. Kennedy Laurie). Giuseppe de Nittis (1846-1884), who came to Florence from Puglia, later, like Boldini, emigrated to Paris. His fine landscape painted before his arrival in Florence (Beach near Barletta) has a breadth and sobriety of execution far removed from the hurried « impressionism » present in his Parisian works. The Gallery's collection of minor Macchiaioli painters and their followers constitutes the most complete and exhaustive documentation of this movement: Raffaello Sernesi (Hills around Florence of 1865), Giuseppe Abbati (Cloister of 1860), Cristiano Banti (Wood-cutter of c. 1861), Adriano Cecioni (Portrait of the artist's wife).
Other Italian schools of the late-nineteenth century are represented by works of their leading artists, such as the Venetian Federigo Zandomeneghi, who painted the fine portrait of Diego Martelli, the art critic (1878), or the Veronese painter Vincenzo Cabianca (studies and landscapes), or Gaetano Previati of Ferrara (On the lawn, 1889-90), Grubicy de Dragon of Milan and Bartolomeo Bezzi of Trento, as well as artists of southern Italy including Filippo Palizzi (Royal Family of Naples hunting), Domenico Morelli (Portrait of Giacomo Tofano) and Antonio Mancini (The mask). Alongside these works are sculptures by artists such as Medardo Rosso of Turin (Man reading, of 1894), the Florentine Adriano Cecioni (collection of plasters), and the neapolitan Vincenzo Gemito (Bust of Giuseppe Verdi). The collection brings us down to the present day, but is limited to Italian art, via the works of Plinio Nomellini (Bacchus) and Galileo Chini (Still-life), Gino Severini and Ardengo Soffici (Tuscan Hill), De Chirico, Casorati, Carena and Rosai, and the sculptures of Andreotti, Viani, Romanelli and Marini. The collections are being constantly expanded by bequests and acquisitions and are in the process of being rearranged, in particular the early nineteenth century section.

The Gallery is constantly acquiring new works, also in the contemporary line, thanks to important bequests, such as that made in 1973 of fifteen paintings by Alberto Magnelli, presented by the artist's widow. Furthermore, the prize works shown at the exhibition of the Premio Nazionale del Fiorino and those presented by the Cenacolo dei Dodici Apostoli to the Gallery of Modern Art provide a record of the continuity and artistic framework of Tuscan civilization.

Ardengo Soffici (Rignano sull'Arno 1879 - Vittoria Apuana 1964), Tuscan Hillside

Alberto Magnelli (Florence 1888 - Meudon 1971): Piano di Rosia

Boboli Gardens

Plan of the Boboli Gardens

1 The Bacchus Fountain - 2 The Buontalenti Grotto - 3 The Goat Grotto - 4 The Caffehaus -
5 The Amphitheatre - 6 The Neptune Fountain - 7 The Cavaliere Garden - 8 The Cyprus
Alley (Viottolone) - 9 The Isolotto and Oceanus Fountain - 10 The Lemon Greenhouse - 11 The
Adam and Eve Grotto 12 The Meridiana Terrace - 13 The Artichoke Fountain

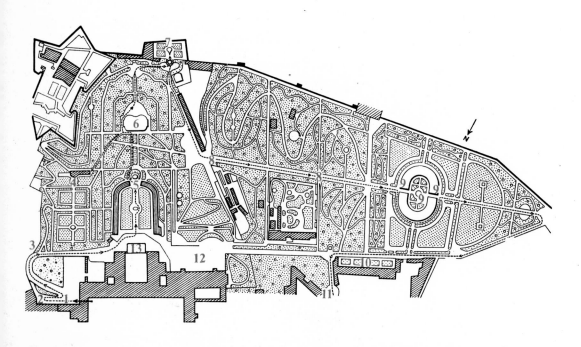

Panorama of Florence from the Boboli Gardens

Bacchus Fountain, or statue of Morgante, dwarf at the court of

Cosimo I, astride a turtle, by Valerio Cioli (late sixteenth century)

The Boboli Gardens are intimately related to the birth and development of the Pitti Palace. When it was acquired by Cosimo I, he immediately planned a large garden, intended as an ideal extension of the palace, on the slopes rising behind it. The same intention was implicit in Ammannati's courtyard which opens out, with its two wings projecting towards the East, forming almost a bridge between the architectural structure in rustic bugnato and the natural setting around. It was logical, therefore, that Ammannati's courtyard was meant to be complemented by the gardens which were then being planned, also on account of its increasing importance as a setting for the entertainments at the Medici court: many memorable festivities and theatrical performances took place in the courtyard, of which the most spectacular were the celebrations in honour of the marriage of Ferdinand I and Christina of Lorraine.

The original plan of the gardens, as recorded in the lunette by Utens (p. 7) was by Tribolo, but it was Bernardo Buontalenti (1536-1608) who realized some of the most spectacular and typically late-Mannerist ideas, for instance, the Grotto (1583-88) named after him, which is a fantastic creation belonging to the taste for the unusual and unexpected characteristic of Florentine art in the second half of the Cinquecento. The Grotto is in a corner of the garden at a small distance from the palace: it is, therefore, slightly off the beaten track and one comes across it almost unexpectedly. The large opening surrounded by icicles of stalactite is surmounted by the coat-of-arms of Ferdinand I and plaques with the signs of the zodiac

Amphitheatre (17th century) with the Artichoke Fountain by Francesco Susini and Francesco del Tadda (1641) in the foreground

Courtyard of the Pitti Palace, architecture by Bartolomeo Ammannati (1558-70)

and flanked by two niches, each containing an allegorical figure by Baccio Bandinelli (1488-1560). Inside, where there were originally thousands of jets and trickles of water running down the walls, one has the impression of a real underground grotto, full of hollows, stalactites and rocks. Only gradually does one realize that among all these imitations of natural forms the artist has designed a strange decoration composed of flocks of sheep and goats with shepherds playing their pipes. The background and vault have fresco paintings by Bernardino Poccetti (1548-1612) which enhance the fantastic character of the grotto with illusionistic scenes of birds and animals seen through the openings in the rocks. On Cosimo I's instructions, the four Prisoners by Michelangelo were placed in the four corners; these statues, which formed part of one of the designs for the tomb of Pope Julius II, are now at the Academy and have been replaced by casts. After passing through a narrow natural arch one comes across a marble group of Paris and Helen by Vincenzo de' Rossi (1525-1587), which conceals the view to another little grotto behind, decorated with wall-fountains in mosaic and a central fountain supporting one of the masterpieces of Florentine Mannerist sculpture: the small Venus by Giambologna (1529-1608) with figures of satyrs gripping onto the basin at her feet. Also Mannerist, but in a humorous vein, is the small marble statue of a dwarf of Cosimo's court, seated naked on a turtle — the so-called Bacchus — above a fountain at the entrance to the Boboli Gardens from the Piazza, by Valerio Cioli (1529-1599). Buontalenti also designed another grotto, the Goat Grotto, in the small secluded garden known as the Garden of Madama, which leads off from

Façade of Buontalenti's Grotto (1583-88)

Internal view of Buontalenti's Grotto (1583-88)

Paris and Helen, marble group by Vincenzo de' Rossi (1560) in the Nymphaeum of Buontalenti's Grotto

Venus leaving her bath, marble statue by Giambologna (1573) in the third recess of Buontalenti's Grotto

the alley to the Theatre: inside, is a stalactite decoration and a group of goats, from which the grotto derives its name. The most important part of the garden, both from the point of view of its complexity and the variety of the structures, fountains and statues decorating it, is that centred on the so-called Theatre and the slope leading up to the fountain of Neptune, from which one has one of the most beautiful panoramas of the city. The Theatre was built from 1618 onwards by Giulio and Alfonso Parigi, who thus transformed the simple Renaissance outline of the gardens into a more complex and articulated design. Consequently, Giambologna's Oceanus fountain was removed from here to the lowest part of the garden, to the so-called Isolotto. The amphitheatre, decorated with steps and niches containing marble statues and ornamental vases, became the setting for famous festivities and performances which the Grand Dukes and their court watched from the central loggia of the palace, overlooking Ammannati's courtyard.

In fact, from this position, the view comprises the semicircle of the « Theatre » (in the centre an obelisk and an antique granite bath from Villa Medici in Rome were added by the Lorraine Grand Dukes in 1841) and continues up the ramp leading to the upper levels of the garden and the Fountain of Neptune (Stoldo Lorenzi, 1565), beyond which towers the gigantic marble statue of Abundance. Counterbalancing this perspective view at the palace end is the Carciofo fountain by Francesco Susini and Francesco del Tadda (1641) which crowns the terrace above the grotto facing on to Ammannati's courtyard. High up on the left is the Fortezza del Belvedere connected to the Boboli Gardens by a gate (at present closed): this upper part of the garden is composed of a large variety of trees and bushes forming an architecture of greenery, with numerous paths and different views onto the city. To the left is the Cafehaus by Zanobi del Rosso (1776), overlooking the lawns and the Ganymede Fountain (XVI century). Above the bastions on the right, is a small villa built in the late seventeenth century called the Villa del Cavaliere, an extremely elegant building which will shortly house the porcelain collections of the Museo degli Argenti.

Walking up towards the right from the Neptune Fountain one reaches the summit of the steep walk known as the Viottolone, edged with double rows of splendid cyprus trees intersected at intervals by marble statues of various periods, which leads down to the lowest part of the garden towards the old city walls and the Porta Romana. To the right and left of the Viottolone the garden stretches out in an infinite number of paths, some of which become tunnels formed by the hedgerows, with fountains and statues at intervals, to create what was known in the sixteenth and seventeenth centuries as the Labyrinth. The Viottolone leads down to one of the most elegant and evocative parts of the garden, the Fountain of Oceanus dominating the Isolotto (small island). This circular complex is surrounded by a tall box hedge with niches cut into it containing statues from the ruined Villa of Pratolino from which they were removed in the early nineteenth century. The design and structure of the Isolotto and the way it is animated by statue groups reflect late-Mannerist taste; it was, in fact, designed and realized by Giulio and Alfonso Parigi from 1618 onwards when the fountain of Oceanus, carved by Giambologna for Francesco I de' Medici in 1576, was removed to this end of the garden. The white marble group composed of the towering figure of Oceanus (replaced by a copy: the original is in the Bargello Museum) with three personifications of rivers at his feet above a marble basin resting on a high base closes the perspective view from the top of the Viottolone. The surrounding pond is also decorated with sculptures in the two semicircles formed by the bridges linking the island to the land, with the figures of Perseus riding Pegasus to free

The Cyprus Alley (« Viottolone »)

Partial view of the « Isolotto » pond, built in 1618 after a design by Giulio Parigi and Alfonso Parigi the Younger

The Oceanus Fountain by Giambologna (1576)

Man emptying a keg into a tub, by Valerio and Simone Cioli (early seventeenth century)

Andromeda from the sea-monster. The balustrade round the pond is decorated in four places with fine and complex sculptural groups of tritons, dolphins, sea-beasts and youths, finishing in basins into which the layout of the south end of the garden beyond the Isolotto, which extends to the Porta Romana, dates principally from the first half of the nineteenth century: Neoclassical in taste are the two columns on plinths terminating in decorative vases which stand within the semicircle formed by huge plane trees and the busts and statues of mythological divinities, while at various points along the walks are groups from Pratolino or removed from other parts of the garden (particularly fine is the small Bacchus by Vincenzo de' Rossi, near to the gate which opens onto the Piazza of Porta Romana). Making one's way back to the Pitti Palace and the « Theatre » along the walk flanking the garden wall, one passes several buildings of the Lorraine period, including the large Limonaia (lemon greenhouse), the small Villa by the Annalena gate, the greenhouses and, at the summit of the path, the fine terrace in front of the Meridiana wing, in which the Lorraine and Savoy rulers had their private apartments: the section of the garden facing the Meridiana was redesigned in the Lorraine period and the slope of the hill decorated with statues and a granite bath in keeping with Neoclassical ideals of English landscape gardening. The Boboli Gardens, therefore, shared the historical changes of the Palace and complete the visit to this rich and varied complex in which artistic beauty harmonizes with that of nature.

Index of Artists

Alessandro Allori (Florence 1535 - 1607): Predella of Holy Martyrs, detail Pitti Palace, Florence, Church of Santo Spirito

Bibliography

F. Inghirami, L'I. e R. Palazzo de' Pitti descritto, Fiesole, 1828
C. Conti, Il Palazzo Pitti, Florence, 1887
Florence, State Archive, Mostra documentaria e iconografica di Palazzo Pitti e del Giardino di Boboli, 1960
A. M. Francini-Ciaranfi, La Galleria Pitti, Catalogue and guide, Florence, 1964
W. Vitzthum, Pietro da Cortona a Palazzo Pitti, Milan, 1965 (with bibl.)
U. Procacci - A. M. Francini-Ciaranfi, La Reggia di Palazzo Pitti, Florence, 1966

M. Chiarini - C. Aschengreen-Piacenti, Artisti alla Corte Granducale, catalogue of the exhibition, Florence, Palazzo Pitti, 1969
C. Aschengreen-Piacenti, Il Museo degli Argenti, Florence, 1969
Id., Capolavori del Museo degli Argenti, Florence, 1969
A. M. Francini-Ciaranfi, La Galleria Pitti, Milan, 1971
F. Gurrieri - J. Chatfield, Boboli Gardens, Florence, 1973

Cover:
Antonio Canova, Venus, 1810, (Carrara marble, height 170 cm.). Palatine Gallery, The Flora Room

© 1973 SCALA
Istituto Fotografico Editoriale, Firenze
Colour Photographs:
SCALA, Firenze
Layout: Giorgio M. Pastafiglia and Fried Rosenstock
Translation:
Françoise Chiarini
Produced by SCALA Istituto Fotografico Editoriale, Firenze
Printed in Italy by
Coop Officine Grafiche Firenze

L. 5.0(
(471